Hate
GROUPS
OPPOSING VIEWPOINTS ®

Mary E. Williams, *Book Editor*

Daniel Leone, *President*
Bonnie Szumski, *Publisher*
Scott Barbour, *Managing Editor*
Helen Cothran, *Senior Editor*

OPPOSING
VIEWPOINTS®
SERIES

GREENHAVEN
PRESS ®

THOMSON
™
GALE

San Diego • Detroit • New York • San Francisco • Cleveland
New Haven, Conn. • Waterville, Maine • London • Munich

LIBRARY OF CONGRESS CATALOGING-IN-PUBLICATION DATA

Hate groups / Mary E. Williams, book editor.
   p. cm. — (Opposing viewpoints series)
   Includes bibliographical references and index.
   ISBN 0-7377-2280-0 (lib. bdg. : alk. paper) —
   ISBN 0-7377-2281-9 (pbk. : alk. paper)
    1. Hate crimes—United States. 2. Arabs—Crimes against—United States.
3. Muslims—Crimes against—United States. 4. Gays—Crimes against—United
States. I. Williams, Mary E., 1960– . II. Opposing viewpoints series (Unnumbered).
HV6773.52.H37 2004
364.15'0973—dc21
                                              2003054324

Printed in the United States of America

"Congress shall make no law...abridging the freedom of speech, or of the press."

First Amendment to the U.S. Constitution

The basic foundation of our democracy is the First Amendment guarantee of freedom of expression. The Opposing Viewpoints Series is dedicated to the concept of this basic freedom and the idea that it is more important to practice it than to enshrine it.

Contents

Why Consider
Opposing Viewpoints?

"The only way in which a human being can make some approach to knowing the whole of a subject is by hearing what can be said about it by persons of every variety of opinion and studying all modes in which it can be looked at by every character of mind. No wise man ever acquired his wisdom in any mode but this."

John Stuart Mill

In our media-intensive culture it is not difficult to find differing opinions. Thousands of newspapers and magazines and dozens of radio and television talk shows resound with differing points of view. The difficulty lies in deciding which opinion to agree with and which "experts" seem the most credible. The more inundated we become with differing opinions and claims, the more essential it is to hone critical reading and thinking skills to evaluate these ideas. Opposing Viewpoints books address this problem directly by presenting stimulating debates that can be used to enhance and teach these skills. The varied opinions contained in each book examine many different aspects of a single issue. While examining these conveniently edited opposing views, readers can develop critical thinking skills such as the ability to compare and contrast authors' credibility, facts, argumentation styles, use of persuasive techniques, and other stylistic tools. In short, the Opposing Viewpoints Series is an ideal way to attain the higher-level thinking and reading skills so essential in a culture of diverse and contradictory opinions.

In addition to providing a tool for critical thinking, Opposing Viewpoints books challenge readers to question their own strongly held opinions and assumptions. Most people form their opinions on the basis of upbringing, peer pressure, and personal, cultural, or professional bias. By reading carefully balanced opposing views, readers must directly confront new ideas as well as the opinions of those with whom they disagree. This is not to simplistically argue that everyone who reads opposing views will—or should—change his or her opinion. Instead, the series enhances readers' understanding of their own views by encouraging confrontation with opposing ideas. Careful examination of others' views can lead to the readers' understanding of the logical inconsistencies in their own opinions, perspective on why they hold an opinion, and the consideration of the possibility that their opinion requires further evaluation.

Evaluating Other Opinions

To ensure that this type of examination occurs, Opposing Viewpoints books present all types of opinions. Prominent spokespeople on different sides of each issue as well as well-known professionals from many disciplines challenge the reader. An additional goal of the series is to provide a forum for other, less known, or even unpopular viewpoints. The opinion of an ordinary person who has had to make the decision to cut off life support from a terminally ill relative, for example, may be just as valuable and provide just as much insight as a medical ethicist's professional opinion. The editors have two additional purposes in including these less known views. One, the editors encourage readers to respect others' opinions—even when not enhanced by professional credibility. It is only by reading or listening to and objectively evaluating others' ideas that one can determine whether they are worthy of consideration. Two, the inclusion of such viewpoints encourages the important critical thinking skill of objectively evaluating an author's credentials and bias. This evaluation will illuminate an author's reasons for taking a particular stance on an issue and will aid in readers' evaluation of the author's ideas.

It is our hope that these books will give readers a deeper understanding of the issues debated and an appreciation of the complexity of even seemingly simple issues when good and honest people disagree. This awareness is particularly important in a democratic society such as ours in which people enter into public debate to determine the common good. Those with whom one disagrees should not be regarded as enemies but rather as people whose views deserve careful examination and may shed light on one's own.

Thomas Jefferson once said that "difference of opinion leads to inquiry, and inquiry to truth." Jefferson, a broadly educated man, argued that "if a nation expects to be ignorant and free . . . it expects what never was and never will be." As individuals and as a nation, it is imperative that we consider the opinions of others and examine them with skill and discernment. The Opposing Viewpoints Series is intended to help readers achieve this goal.

David L. Bender and Bruno Leone,
Founders

Greenhaven Press anthologies primarily consist of previously published material taken from a variety of sources, including periodicals, books, scholarly journals, newspapers, government documents, and position papers from private and public organizations. These original sources are often edited for length and to ensure their accessibility for a young adult audience. The anthology editors also change the original titles of these works in order to clearly present the main thesis of each viewpoint and to explicitly indicate the opinion presented in the viewpoint. These alterations are made in consideration of both the reading and comprehension levels of a young adult audience. Every effort is made to ensure that Greenhaven Press accurately reflects the original intent of the authors included in this anthology.

Introduction

"The militant [hate] groups are worth studying . . .
because they let us see white racism in its unfiltered,
unguarded form."

—Raphael S. Ezekiel

Several high-profile hate crimes of the past decade have drawn the public's attention to white supremacist groups such as the Ku Klux Klan, racist skinhead gangs, and various neo-Nazi organizations. Membership in the Klan, America's oldest and best-known white supremacist group, has waxed and waned over the years. The Klan, which began in 1865 as a southern vigilante group that threatened and terrorized former slaves, currently shares the Nazi disdain for Jews, non-whites, and homosexuals. However, many observers are more concerned about neo-Nazi organizations, which, with the help of the Internet, have proliferated since the 1980s. Some social analysts see neo-Nazi groups as an evolving threat due to their appeal to educated middle-class youths and because of their developing relationship with hate groups in Europe.

Nazism, in fact, originated in Europe with the rise of Adolf Hitler's Brown Shirts and the National Socialist Party in Germany after World War I. Hitler's endorsement of fascism and anti-Semitism influenced several prominent leaders of the American far right in the 1930s, including William Dudley Pelley, who founded the Silver Shirts in 1933. Modeled after Hitler's Brown Shirts, this organization collaborated with the pro-Nazi German American Bund and trained its members for armed insurrection. Pelley's group was just one among dozens of small extremist groups that emerged to confront what they believed was a worldwide conspiracy among Jews to take control of every nation. Pelley and others maintained that an ultrasecret Jewish government would attempt to rise to power by covertly pitting gentiles against each other, and they blamed Jews for most of the social and political ills of the time.

At the end of World War II, Wesley Swift, a Protestant minister influenced by Pelley's ideas, founded the Church of

Jesus Christ Christian in Lancaster, California. Swift championed an American variation of British-Israelism, a nineteenth-century doctrine claiming that the Anglo-Saxon-Celtic people are the true descendants of the biblical lost tribes of Israel. In the United States, under the influence of Swift and other clergymen who believed in the worldwide Jewish conspiracy, British-Israelism evolved into a quasi-religious sect known as Christian Identity. The basic tenets of Christian Identity include the notion that nonwhites are soulless beings created before humans and that Jews are the offspring of the devil. Identity followers contend that white "Aryans" are the true descendants of Adam and Eve and that miscegenation is the "original sin" that brought evil into the world. Identity adherents also maintain that the world is on the verge of a final battle between good and evil, with Aryans battling Jews in order to bring about Christ's kingdom on Earth.

In the latter twentieth century, several groups emerged as outgrowths and affiliates of Wesley Swift's Church of Jesus Christ Christian. After Swift's death in 1970, Lockheed Aircraft engineer Richard Butler took charge of the church. He then moved to northern Idaho in 1973 to establish Aryan Nations, a new Christian Identity organization headquartered near Hayden Lake. Butler set up a twenty-acre compound, complete with a church-school and a paramilitary training facility, which became a gathering place for militant white supremacists during the 1980s and 1990s. Starting in 1982, Aryan Nations held annual congresses in which skinheads, Klansmen, and neo-Nazis would congregate to learn about white supremacist politics and culture.

A popular item at these Aryan Nations conferences was a book entitled *The Turner Diaries* by Andrew MacDonald, a pseudonym for William Pierce. Pierce had been a publicist for the post–World War II American Nazi Party before forming the neo-Nazi National Alliance in the late 1960s. Pierce's novel, an account of an underground Aryan organization that uses terrorism to overthrow the U.S. government, is thought to have inspired Timothy McVeigh to bomb the Oklahoma City federal building in April 1995, killing 168 people.

Another organization with connections to Aryan Nations and Christian Identity is Tom Metzger's White Aryan Resistance (WAR). Metzger was ordained as a Christian Identity minister in 1975, but he abandoned this ministry to open his own Klan chapter in 1981. As part of what he called "a deliberate move to scare off the weak-kneed people from my group," Metzger broke with the Klan and established WAR in 1984. With the help of his son, John, he sought out recruits from among the growing number of U.S. skinheads. According to researcher Mark S. Hamm, author of *American Skinheads*, Metzger aimed to "inject some ideology into the skinheads" and to strengthen "the emerging global struggle of whites against Jews and mongrels." He orchestrated a campaign involving computer links, phone hot lines, and media appearances that drew national attention in the late 1980s. Metzger's followers were seen on several popular talk shows, including an appearance on *The Geraldo Rivera Show* that escalated into a violent televised brawl.

Unlike Metzger, Ben Klassen, the original founder of the World Church of the Creator, never had any connections with Christian Identity. Klassen argued that the white race was the finest achievement of nature and that hatred of Jews and people of color was a natural result of loving the white race. He held no allegiance to God or Christianity, claiming that such concepts were deplorable because they were derived from Judaism. Klassen committed suicide in 1993, but his group was reorganized by Illinois law student Matthew Hale in 1996. Under Hale's leadership, the World Church of the Creator— recently renamed the Creativity Movement—has become one of the most prominent neo-Nazi groups in the United States. According to the Southern Poverty Law Center (SPLC), an organization that monitors hate groups, Creativity has several hundred hard-core members and "thousands of affiliated members" who read its literature, join its Internet chat rooms, and subscribe to its theories. Although the group claims to disdain religion, its battle cry is "RAHOWA," or Racial Holy War—a phrase signifying belief in the necessity of an apocalyptic race war to bring about white rule.

Examining the history and objectives of these neo-Nazi groups reveals why some analysts believe they constitute a danger to America. But recent developments also suggest that the militant white supremacist movement has been weakened and faces an uncertain future. In 1990 the SPLC won a $12.5-million civil suit against WAR's Tom Metzger in the case of an Ethiopian immigrant who had been murdered by skinheads. Metzger was declared liable because he had originally recruited the skinheads and had encouraged them to participate in violent behavior against nonwhites. In 2000 Idaho residents who had been shot at by security guards for the Aryan Nations were awarded $6.3 million in damages. Aryan Nations founder, Richard Butler, was then forced to hand over his group's land, which now serves as an environmental lab. In 2002 National Alliance leader William Pierce died, leaving rival members fighting for control of the organization, and in January 2003, Creativity leader Hale was arrested on charges of solicitation for murder.

Even without the setbacks posed by lawsuits, deaths, and arrests, many experts maintain that hate groups cannot seriously endanger a society that values tolerance and diversity. Others caution, however, that Americans should not underestimate the potential for bias crimes and domestic terrorism among hate-group members. These and other concerns are explored in the following chapters of *Hate Groups: Opposing Viewpoints:* Are Hate Crimes a Serious Problem? What Motivates People to Hate? Do Certain Groups Pose a Threat to Tolerance? How Should Society Respond to Hate Groups? This volume provides an array of opinions on how society should confront bias-motivated crimes and extremist subcultures.

CHAPTER 1

Are Hate Crimes a Serious Problem?

Chapter Preface

A series of brutal hate crimes—offenses triggered by hatred of persons based on their color, ethnicity, religion, or sexual orientation—drew national attention in the late 1990s. In May 1998 a group of black men and teenagers beat Mark Dale Butts, a white man, to death after a racially charged exchange in a Colorado bar. One month later three white men flogged black hitchhiker James Byrd Jr. until he was unable to move, chained his ankles to their truck's back bumper, and dragged him until his body was torn into pieces. In the fall of that same year, gay college student Matthew Shepard died after being lured from a campus bar, pistol-whipped, tied to a fence, and abandoned in near-freezing temperatures. Then during the 1999 Fourth of July weekend, neo-Nazi Benjamin Smith went on a shooting spree in Indiana and Illinois, killing an African American and a Korean American and wounding nine others before turning his gun on himself. The following month, white supremacist Buford Furrow injured several children and a receptionist when he opened fire on a Jewish community center in southern California. He shot and killed a Filipino American postal worker later that same day.

This apparent surge in hate crimes continued into the twenty-first century, when a growing number of immigrants—particularly Asian and Arab Americans—became the victims of bias-motivated assaults. In the year after the terrorist attacks of September 11, 2001, for example, the FBI reported that hate crimes against Arabs and those perceived as Middle Eastern increased by more than 1500 percent. Morris Dees, trial counsel for the Southern Poverty Law Center, says that he is concerned by what appears to be the increasing frequency and viciousness of bias attacks, which are committed by both whites and minorities. Moreover, he states, "Much of the hatred is fueled by the growing number of organized hate groups and the proliferation of Internet sites devoted to racism, anti-Semitism, homophobia and other forms of intolerance."

Other analysts, however, dispute the claim that hate crimes are becoming more brutal and frequent. For one thing, the intensive media coverage surrounding the murders of James

Byrd and Matthew Shepard may have created the impression that the incidence of *violent* hate crimes increased during the past decade. As columnist James Lacey points out, "When people hear the term 'hate crime' they almost immediately get an image of the vilest assaults. People may have an image of hate represented by Byrd being dragged behind a truck, but the reality is that most hate crimes are far more prosaic. If a person gets upset at an ethnic Arab and tells him to go back to his own country, for the purposes of the [FBI] record that is as much a hate crime as if he goes out at night looking for Arabs to beat to death." While verbal attacks are troubling, classifying them as hate crimes creates skewed statistics that can lead people to wrongly conclude that murderous bigotry is on the increase, Lacey asserts. In actuality, he maintains, blatant prejudice and bigotry have decreased over the course of America's history.

The debate over how hate crimes are defined, recorded, and reported is addressed by the authors in the following chapter. While some contend that such crimes are on the rise, others believe their prevalence is exaggerated by the media.

"There has been a noticeable rise in hate violence against Muslims across the nation."

Hate Crimes Against Arabs and Muslims Are Increasing

Earl Ofari Hutchinson

Since the terrorist attacks of September 11, 2001, hate crimes against Muslims and Arabs have increased, writes Earl Ofari Hutchinson in the following viewpoint. Authorities, however, often treat these bias-motivated attacks as regular crimes, causing an undercount in the occurrence of hate crimes and leading the public to believe that such crimes are rare or nonexistent. The FBI and police should take the threat of hate crimes as seriously as they take the threat of terrorism, the author concludes. Hutchinson is a columnist and the author of *The Crisis in Black and Black*.

As you read, consider the following questions:

1. What facts suggest that the murder of Egyptian-American grocer Adel Karpas was a hate crime, in Hutchinson's opinion?
2. According to the author, who is responsible for record-keeping on hate crimes?
3. In Hutchinson's view, why do authorities avoid labeling bias-motivated crimes as hate crimes?

Earl Ofari Hutchinson, "Hate in the News: A Jarring Reminder on Hate Crimes," www.tolerance.org, September 19, 2002. Copyright © 2002 by Earl Ofari Hutchinson. Reproduced by permission of Alternet.

M uslim and civil liberties groups repeatedly warned that they would be scapegoated for the September 11, 2001, terror attacks. They were right.

A recent report from the L.A. [Los Angeles, California] County Human Relations Commission confirmed that hate attacks against Muslims . . . surged [between 2001 and 2002]. The big jump in L.A. County hate attacks is no aberration. The FBI noted there has been a noticeable rise in hate violence against Muslims across the nation. . . .

Despite the danger, many police agencies still bury their heads in the sand and deny hate violence is a serious threat, or even exists. The murder of an Egyptian-American grocer, Adel Karpas, in his store was a troubling example of the mixed uncertainty and confusion of police on hate violence. L.A. County sheriffs found no evidence hate was the motive in his slaying.

But even if sheriff's officials are right and the murder was nothing more than a vicious, stupid, and bungled robbery attempt, the fact that Karpas was slain four days after September 11 and no money was taken at least raises a good possibility that his ethnicity—and not a grab at the store's cash register—was the reason for his murder.

Downplaying Hate Crimes

However, it's simply often easier for police officials to treat crimes, such as the Karpas tragedy, as a common crime rather than a hate crime. This avoids the sticky and potentially volatile risk of inflaming racial tensions. But the L.A. County Sheriff's Department, which has one of the more active hate crimes units in the nation, initially at least did not reflexively discount hate as a possible motive in Karmas' killing. Many other police departments would have.

There are still hundreds of them that refuse to report hate crimes, or to label racially motivated hate crimes as such. If President [George W.] Bush and Attorney General John Ashcroft hadn't publicly pledged to crack down on hate attacks against Muslims, police officials in cities where Muslims and Sikhs were murdered, assaulted and their mosques burned after 9/11 would not have automatically labeled these attacks as hate crimes—and FBI officials might not have directed their local agents to vigorously pursue them as such.

The ignoring or downplaying of hate crimes by many police agencies gets worse each year. According to a report by Human Rights Watch, fewer police agencies reported hate crimes to the FBI in 2000 than in 1999. And the number that reported them in 1999 dropped from those reporting in 1998.

Parker. © 2001 by *Florida Today*. Reprinted by permission of Jeff Parker.

The indifference by many police agencies to hate crimes insures federal officials can't accurately gauge the magnitude of hate violence. This lulls the public into thinking hate crimes have diminished or are non-existent.

Federal Culpability

While the police agencies bear some of the blame for this laxity in reporting, so do federal officials. When Congress passed the Hate Crimes Statistics Act of 1990, it compelled the FBI to collect figures on hate violence. However, it did not compel police agencies to report them. Record keeping on hate crimes is still left up to the discretion of local police chiefs and city officials.

Many don't bother compiling them because they regard hate crimes as a politically loaded minefield that can tarnish their image and create even more racial friction. They see no need to allocate more resources to enable police to recognize and combat hate violence. And unlike the L.A. County Sheriff's Department, many police agencies in America haven't established hate task force units, or set specific procedures for dealing with hate crimes.

The Hate Crimes Prevention Act of 1998 was supposed to close these loopholes and increase the types of hate crimes prosecuted and the penalties for them. But the measure has been repeatedly stonewalled in the Senate.

With Congress fixated on passing and bank-rolling Bush's homeland security bill, and much of the public more willing than ever to green light racial profiling and soft pedal, if not scrap, civil liberties protections, as long as the target is Arab Americans, expanded hate crimes legislation is dead in the water.[1]

Even as Bush and Ashcroft talked tough and condemned the hate attacks against Muslims, they did absolutely nothing to prod Congress to pass the bill. They have given no indication they will change.

The surge in hate violence is a jarring reminder that some, in their bigoted and misguided zeal, see it as their right and duty to attack Muslims—and anyone else who doesn't fit their definition of what a patriotic American is. FBI and police agencies should make nailing them the same high priority they make nailing foreign terrorists in America.

---

1. The Homeland Security Bill, which expands the federal government's power to collect information regarding security risks, was signed into law in November 2002.

> *"In the year after Sept. 11, 2001, only a small fraction of a percent of Arabs and Muslims reported being victims of hate."*

The Prevalence of Hate Crimes Against Arabs and Muslims Is Exaggerated

James Lacey

In the following viewpoint, James Lacey disputes the contention that hate crimes against Arabs and Muslims have greatly increased since the terrorist attacks of September 11, 2001. For one thing, Lacey argues, hate crime statistics are politically biased and do not truly reflect how many crimes are motivated by bigotry. Moreover, he points out, Arabs had been racially classified as white prior to the terrorist attacks. Since crimes against whites are not typically classified as hate crimes, it's possible that anti-Arab assaults had been undercounted before 2001. But even given this undercount, Lacey concludes, a very small percentage of the U.S. Arab and Muslim population has been attacked. Lacey is a columnist and a colonel in the U.S. Army Reserve.

As you read, consider the following questions:

1. In Lacey's opinion, what incidents reveal the arbitrary way in which hate crimes are defined?
2. How many anti-Arab hate crimes were recorded in 2002, according to the author?
3. What group of people benefit from the use of hate-crime statistics, in Lacey's view?

James Lacey, "Hate Crime Statistics Distort Truth of American Tolerance," *Insight*, vol. 19, January 7, 2003, p. 50. Copyright © 2003 by News World Communications, Inc. Reproduced by permission.

Recently released FBI hate-crime data show that crimes against Arabs and Muslims have increased more than 1,500 percent [since 2002]. Presumably this seeming outpouring of ethnic hatred is related directly to the aftereffects of [the terrorist attacks of September 11, 2001]. Our shock at that terrible tragedy apparently has created a desire to lash out at innocents who bear a resemblance to the monsters who attacked us.

However, before we drown ourselves in self-recrimination, some perspective is required. It does not take too much peering behind the numbers to show that rather than a nation wracked with hate, we are a people of remarkable forbearance.

Before we look at those numbers though, it needs to be pointed out that hate-crime statistics are politically stacked and arbitrary. They require law-enforcement agencies to look past the crime and determine a person's intent and motivation. It is not enough to say Person A murdered Person B and prosecute accordingly. Now police must determine whether Person B was selected for murder (or any other crime) because he/she was of a different race, ethnicity, religion or sexual orientation than Person A.

A Judgment Call

Determining what constitutes a hate crime leads to all manner of logical absurdities. For instance: Did a black thief target a white person for robbery because he is white, or did he study the latest socioeconomic data and see that by robbing a white person he is more likely to maximize his potential income? The first would be a hate crime. The second would not.

Because determining a hate crime most often is a judgment call, it allows prejudice and political correctness to enter into the equation. When three white men chained [black man] James Byrd to a truck and dragged him to his death the incident was classified as a hate crime, which it surely was. However, when Colin Ferguson, a black man, boarded a Long Island Railroad train and systematically murdered six whites and wounded 19 others, it was not classified as a hate crime, despite Ferguson's long history of antiwhite outbursts.

In 2001, the FBI recorded 1.7 million acts of interracial violent crime. Of that figure, 1.1 million were cases of blacks committing violent crimes on whites. Despite this, the FBI finds that blacks suffer three times as many hate crimes as whites and as a percentage of the population are almost 30 times more likely to be targeted for a hate crime. Somehow the FBI has peered into the minds of those who committed the 1.1 million acts of black-on-white crime and determined that there was no racial motivation behind them. That is ridiculous.

What Do the Numbers Mean?

Assuming, for now, that law enforcement is equipped with a magical clairvoyance that allows it to look into the hearts of criminals, what then do the numbers tell us?

The 1,500 percent increase in hate crimes against Arabs and Muslims represents 481 actual crimes—up from 28 the year before. Since Arabs previously had been classified as whites, there really is no way to tell if the surge is as great as it appears or if there is just a new sensitivity that allows Arabs to be broken out into a distinct new subset, which no one bothered to do before. In other words, there also may have been 481 hate crimes against Arabs the previous year, but the number was rolled into the larger total, and therefore hidden.

A Hate Crime Epidemic

The Los Angeles County Human Relations Commission's 1999 "Hate Crimes Report" claimed that hate crimes in the county had risen 11.7% from the previous year. The announcement led to a bevy of headlines and newscasts, giving the impression that the county was experiencing a hate crime epidemic. The commission warned that the rising number of crimes "erodes the public's perception that schools, places of business and homes are safe environments, protected from hate crime."

A close look at the statistics, however, shows that in this county of 10 million people, the most polyglot population on the face of the earth, the number of alleged—that's alleged, mind you—hate crimes for 1999 was 859. These were incidents reported by police, activist groups and schools. Of that total, 98 resulted in felony charges, and 102 were cases against juveniles. To be sure, one true hate crime is too many. But as crime waves go, this one seemed more like a ripple.

Fred Dickey, *Los Angeles Times Magazine*, October 22, 2000.

It also is important to keep in mind what constitutes a hate crime as we consider the "crisis" of hate that Arab-Americans are facing. When people hear the term "hate crime" they almost immediately get an image of the vilest assaults. People may have an image of hate represented by Byrd being dragged behind a truck, but the reality is that most hate crimes are far more prosaic. If a person gets upset at an ethnic Arab and tells him to go back to his own country, for purposes of the record that is as much a hate crime as if he goes out at night looking for Arabs to beat to death.

Still, 481 acts of ethnic hatred are 481 too many. But before the national castigation begins, that number needs to be examined from a new viewpoint. There are more than 3 million Americans of Arab descent (some estimates areas high as 6 million). This means that 0.016 percent of them were victims of a hate crime [in 2002]. This is about the same probability as being hit by lightning in a lifetime. Jews, by comparison, have a 0.019 percent chance of being the victim of a hate crime, which is almost double the chance of a black being the victim.

Whites suffered only 891 hate crimes (0.008 percent) [in 2002], but as we have seen, that number is suspect. For instance, the whites killed by hate-filled Arab fanatics on Sept. 11 were not classified as victims of a hate crime. Does the fact that the terrorists were targeting Americans in general or that members of other ethnic groups also were killed somehow mitigate the hatred felt toward any particular group?

The happy fact is that while there still is hatred in the United States it is dwarfed by the good will and generous spirit of most Americans. In what other country could members of one ethnic group inflict such an incredible blow on a nation and the response be so muted? In the year after Sept. 11, 2001, only a small fraction of a percent of Arabs and Muslims reported being victims of hate. Out of approximately 3 million Arabs in the United States, 2,999,519 of them went about their lives without reporting the slightest bit of harassment. Americans can be justly proud of the tolerance that has been exhibited in the face of so terrible a disaster.

As a side note, the FBI should get out of the mind-reading business. A crime is a crime is a crime, and justice should be applied accordingly. Hate-crime statistics are good only for feeding into the propaganda of race-baiting hatemongers who make their living inflaming racial and ethnic animosity.

"Lesbian, gay and bisexual Americans are frequent targets of vicious hate crimes."

Antigay Hate Crimes Are a Serious Problem

Human Rights Campaign

The Human Rights Campaign (HRC) is a nonprofit organization that seeks to protect the civil rights of gay, lesbian, bisexual, and transgendered Americans. In the following viewpoint the HRC maintains that gays, lesbians, bisexuals, and people perceived as homosexual are frequently the victims of bias-motivated attacks. These assaults are often exceptionally violent, the authors point out—and intended to "send a message" to the gay community that homosexuals will not be tolerated. Currently, however, most federal laws only allow the prosecution of hate crimes based on race, color, religion, or national origin. The HRC concludes that sexual orientation must be covered by hate crime laws to ensure that all hate crime victims receive federal assistance.

As you read, consider the following questions:
1. According to the HRC, why are hate crimes underreported to the police?
2. How many antigay bias incidents were reported by the National Coalition of Anti-Violence Programs in 1999, according to the HRC?
3. What two federal hate crime statutes include sexual orientation as a category? Why are these statutes inadequate, in the authors' opinion?

L esbian, gay and bisexual Americans are frequent targets of vicious hate crimes. Only in rare circumstances, however, can the federal government help in investigating and prosecuting hate crimes committed against someone because of his or her real or perceived sexual orientation. Thus, federal law enforcement authorities cannot assist in anti-gay hate crimes—as they do in hate crimes based on race, color, religion or national origin. The Human Rights Campaign (HRC) advocates for adding actual or perceived gender, sexual orientation and disability to laws governing prosecution of hate crimes. HRC believes that hate crimes based on sexual orientation should be investigated and prosecuted on an equal basis as other categories of hate crimes now covered by state and federal law.

All violent crimes are reprehensible. But the damage done by hate crimes cannot be measured solely in terms of physical injury or dollars and cents. Hate crimes rend the fabric of our society and fragment communities because they target a whole group and not just the individual victim. Hate crimes are committed to make an entire community fearful. A violent hate crime is intended to "send a message" that a person and his or her "kind" will not be tolerated—many times leaving the victim and others in their group feeling isolated, vulnerable and unprotected. Eighty-five percent of law enforcement officials recently surveyed say they recognize this type of violence to be more serious than similar crimes not motivated by bias, according to a study funded by the U.S. Department of Justice's Bureau of Justice Statistics.

Further, statistics support that gay, lesbian, and bisexual Americans are often targeted for violence. Under the Hate Crimes Statistics Act, the Federal Bureau of Investigation consistently reports that hate crimes based on sexual orientation are the third highest reported category of hate crimes—behind race and religion, respectively. The category of sexual orientation is not currently included in any federal criminal civil rights laws. In addition, many gays and lesbians are not "out" to their families, coworkers or friends, and thus they believe they have no one to seek assistance from or even discuss their experience with hate-motivated violence.

Hate crimes are often inordinately severe, sometimes going well beyond the force needed even to kill someone. For example, a gay man died after being stabbed 35 times during a recent hate crime in Texas.

Hate Crimes Are Underreported

Law enforcement experts agree that when compared to other crimes, hate crimes are underreported to the police. Minority groups, including gays and lesbians, historically have had strained relations with law enforcement officials and fear what is called "re-victimization," whereby the officials verbally or physically attack the person who reports the crime. They fear that officials also may blame them, and be unwilling to write up a report.

Researchers found that only one-third of victims of anti-gay hate crimes reported the incident to police, as compared to 57 percent of the victims of random crimes, according to a study funded by the National Institute of Mental Health. It found that many victims of anti-gay incidents do not report the crimes to local law enforcement officials because they fear their sexual orientation may be made public—to family, employers and others—or they fear they will receive insensitive or hostile treatment, including physical abuse. The National Bias Crimes Training for Law Enforcement and Victim Assistance Professionals calls this phenomena "secondary injury"—the victim's perceived rejection by, and lack of, expected support from the community.

An example of this occurred as a result of the bombing of the predominantly lesbian bar in Atlanta in February 1997. Five bar patrons were injured severely enough to be taken to the hospital by ambulance. However, one victim who had a shrapnel wound refused to be treated when she saw reporters in the hospital emergency room.

In addition, people are less motivated to report hate crimes to authorities in those jurisdictions where no hate crime laws covering sexual orientation exist. If a perpetrator cannot be prosecuted, victims may consider it a waste of time and energy to report the crime.

Although hate crimes based on sexual orientation are underreported, the number of hate crimes reported suggests an appalling amount of bias-motivated violence against gays and lesbians. As overall serious crime continued to decrease for the eighth consecutive year, hate crimes based on sexual orientation have continued to rise and increased 4.5 percent from 1998 to 1999, according to the FBI's Uniform Crime Reports. Reported hate crime incidents based on sexual orientation have more than tripled since the FBI began collecting statistics in 1991—comprising 16.7 percent of all hate crimes for 1999 at 1,317. Hate crimes based on sexual orientation continue to make up the third highest category after race and religion, which make up 54.5 and 17.9 percent, respectively of the total, 7,876.

Evidence indicates that FBI data does not paint the whole picture, however. The National Coalition of Anti-Violence Programs, a private organization that tracks bias incidents against gay, lesbian, bisexual and transgender people, reported 1,965 incidents in 1999 in 25 cities/jurisdictions across the country while the FBI collected 1,317 incidents from 12,122 reporting agencies for the year.

Inadequate Statutes

Only 25 states and the District of Columbia now have hate crime laws that include "sexual orientation" in the list of protected categories. Forty-five states have hate crimes laws, but their listing of categories do not all include "sexual orientation." Six states have no hate crimes laws whatsoever.

In May 1997, South Carolina Attorney General Charles Condon drafted a hate crime bill for the state in response to the burning of numerous African-American churches there. The draft bill did not include sexual orientation because, according to Condon's legislative lobbyist, "Nobody has demonstrated to us that there's a problem [with people being attacked because of their sexual orientation], so we decided to take action against race-based hate crimes." However, there were at least four documented reports of anti-gay hate crimes in the state in the previous year. A hate crime victim from South Carolina also testified before the Senate Judiciary Committee in June 1997 about a violent beating that occurred in April 1996 that left him without hearing in one ear, broken ribs, and 47 stitches in his face. The perpetrators yelled, "We're going to get you, faggot," he said. He was left for dead in a trash bin outside a primarily hetero-sexual bar in Myrtle Beach, S.C.

Currently, only two federal hate crime statutes include the category of sexual orientation:

The Hate Crimes Statistics Act (PL 101-275) became law in 1990 and was reauthorized in 1996. This law requires the FBI to collect statistics on hate crimes on the basis of race, re-ligion, ethnicity, sexual orientation and disability. Although the FBI is required to collect and analyze the statistics from local and state law enforcement agencies, the local and state agencies are *not* required to provide statistics to the FBI. This law does not allow federal assistance in investigation and prosecution of hate crimes or enhance penalties for hate crime perpetrators; it simply compiles statistics from the var-ious local and state jurisdictions that report to the FBI.

Why People Commit Hate Crimes

Most hate crimes are carried out by otherwise law-abiding young people who see little wrong with their actions. Alco-hol and drugs sometimes help fuel these crimes, but the main determinant appears to be personal prejudice, a situation that colors people's judgment, blinding the aggressors to the immorality of what they are doing. Such prejudice is most likely rooted in an environment that disdains someone who is "different" or sees that difference as threatening. One ex-pression of this prejudice is the perception that society sanc-tions attacks on certain groups. For example, Dr. Karen Franklin, a forensic psychology fellow at the Washington In-stitute for Mental Illness Research and Training, has found that, in some settings, offenders perceive that they have so-cietal permission to engage in violence against homosexuals.

American Psychological Association, *APA Monitor*, 1998.

The Hate Crimes Sentencing Enhancement Act (PL 103-322) was passed as a part of the Violent Crime Control and Law Enforcement Act of 1994. This law directs the U.S. Sentencing Commission to provide sentencing enhance-ments of "not less than three offense levels for offenses that the finder of fact at trial determines beyond a reasonable doubt are hate crimes." This law is considered the federal counterpart to state hate crime penalty statutes, to be used for hate crimes committed on *only* federal property, such as national parks. Because the law can only be used when a crime is perpetrated on federal property, it is very rarely used.

Support for New Legislation

A broad coalition of groups, including 175 civil rights, civic, religious, state and local government associations and law enforcement organizations, supports legislation to amend current federal criminal civil rights law under the Civil Rights Act of 1968 (18 U.S.C. 245). These changes would provide authority for federal officials to investigate and prosecute cases in which the violence occurs because of a victim's actual or perceived gender, sexual orientation and disability, and would eliminate an overly restrictive jurisdictional obstacle to prosecution. This legislation, the Hate Crimes Prevention Act, was originally introduced in 1997 after a White House Conference on Hate Crimes.

Since then, the majority of lawmakers in the U.S. Congress voted in support of the legislation when a revised version, the Local Law Enforcement Enhancement Act, was offered as an amendment to the Senate Department of Defense Authorization bill in June 2000. The bill passed the Senate in a bipartisan vote, 57 to 42, including 13 Republicans. In September 2000, the House passed a motion to instruct in support of the measure, 232 to 192, including 41 Republicans. Despite these strong votes, opponents of the legislation were able to strip the bill from the Defense Department bill before the end of the 106th Congress. The bill was reintroduced in the 107th Congress with a record number of original cosponsors (S. 625/H.R. 1343). HRC supports this bill and will work for its passage. [As this volume goes to press, no new federal hate crime bills have been signed into law.]

Achieving Justice

18 U.S.C. 245 is one of the primary statutes used to combat racial and religious violence. The statute currently prohibits intentional interference with enjoyment of a federal right or benefit, such as attending school or being employed, on the basis of the victim's race, religion, national origin or color.

Under this statute, the government must prove the crime occurred because of the victim's race (or other protected category) and because he or she was enjoying a specifically enumerated federally protected right. These dual requirements have severely restricted the ability of the federal government to act in appropriate cases.

State and local authorities have played, and will continue to play, the primary role in investigating and prosecuting hate violence. But federal jurisdiction would provide an important backstop to ensure that justice is achieved in every case. The Local Law Enforcement Enhancement Act limits the federal government's jurisdiction to only the most serious violent crimes directed at persons, resulting in death or bodily injury, and not property crimes. This measure would allow states with inadequate resources to take advantage of Justice Department resources and personnel in limited cases that have been authorized by the attorney general. And it enables federal, state and local authorities to work together as partners in the investigation and prosecution of bias-related crimes.

*"The mainstream media is guilty of pro-gay
bias."*

The Media Exaggerate the Problem of Antigay Hate Crimes

Andrew Sullivan

The prevalence of antigay hate crimes has been overstated in the mainstream media, argues Andrew Sullivan in the following viewpoint. The 1998 murder of gay college student Matthew Shepard, for example, received extensive media coverage, while the 1999 rape and murder of a youth by two gay men was virtually ignored by major newspapers. Moreover, a close examination of hate-crime statistics reveals that only two or three gay-specific murders occur each year, Sullivan points out. The mainstream media, however, hype the problem of antigay attacks to help fulfill the agenda of interest groups seeking to include sexual orientation in hate-crime laws, the author claims. Sullivan is a senior editor of the *New Republic* and a contributing writer to the *New York Times Magazine*.

As you read, consider the following questions:

1. What was Sullivan's initial reaction to claims by right-wingers that the major media have a pro-gay bias?
2. How many news stories about Matthew Shepard appeared in the month after his death, according to the author?
3. In Sullivan's opinion, what is ironic about the fact that gay rights activists ignored the murder of Jesse Dirkhising?

What happened on September 26, 1999, to 13-year-old Jesse Dirkhising can only be described as evil. Two men who had become friendly with Jesse and his family invited the boy over for the day. According to prosecutors at the trial [in 2001] in Bentonville, Arkansas, the two men drugged Jesse, tied him to a bed, shoved his underwear into his mouth to gag him, added duct tape to silence him, raped him for hours using a variety of objects, including food, and then left him in such a position on the bed that he slowly suffocated to death.

Unless you frequent rabid right-wing sites on the Internet or read the *Washington Times*, you've probably never heard of this case. The *New York Times* has yet to run a single story about it. The *Washington Post* has run only a tiny Associated Press report—and an ombudsman's explanation of why no further coverage is merited. Among certain, mainly gay-hating right-wingers, the discrepancy between the coverage of this case and the wall-to-wall coverage of the similarly horrifying murder of Matthew Shepard[1] proves beyond any doubt that the mainstream media is guilty of pro-gay bias.

Do they have a point? My first, defensive, reaction was no. And reading the accounts from some right-wing outlets, any gay person would be defensive. Some on the far right clearly want to use this case to raise vicious canards about gay men. They want to argue that this pedophilic rape-murder is representative of the "homosexual lifestyle" and to wield it as a weapon against the notion of gay equality and dignity as a whole. A similar argument was made recently by Mary Eberstadt in the *Weekly Standard*, a magazine that never misses an opportunity to demean and disparage homosexuals. In two lengthy articles she asserted that pedophilia is an increasingly prominent part of gay life and is condoned by gay leaders. For Michelle Malkin, writing in the right-wing *Jewish World Review*, the Dirkhising case is evidence of Eberstadt's thesis: "The defense of gay pedophilia has metastasized deep and far into the national conscience."

This is ugly nonsense. There's no credible evidence that

---

1. In 1998 gay college student Matthew Shepard died after being brutally beaten by two men he had met in a Wyoming bar.

gay culture is more accepting of pedophilia than it was, say, 20 or 100 years ago. On the contrary, while pedophilia has always been a vile undercurrent in some gay circles (as in some straight circles), the vast majority of homosexuals are rightly horrified by the sexual abuse of children.

Evidence of Media Bias

But, difficult as it may be to admit, some of the gay-baiting right's argument about media bias holds up. Consider the following statistics. In the month after Shepard's murder, Nexis recorded 3,007 stories about his death. In the month after Dirkhising's murder. Nexis recorded 46 stories about his. In all of [2000], only one article about Dirkhising appeared in a major mainstream newspaper, the *Boston Globe*. The *New York Times* and the *Los Angeles Times* ignored the incident completely. In the same period, the *New York Times* published 45 stories about Shepard, and the *Washington Post* published 28. This discrepancy isn't just real. It's staggering.

In the *Washington Post*, a news editor argued that the paper covers only crimes that are local, inflame local opinion, or have national policy implications. The Shepard story was news in a way the Dirkhising story wasn't because it "prompted debate on hate crimes and the degree to which there is still intolerance of gay people in this country. It was much more than a murder story for us." But wasn't the media's instant blanket coverage part of the reason for the debate? If the Dirkhising murder had been covered instantly with the same attention to gruesome detail, wouldn't it, too, have prompted a national conversation?

You might argue that the Shepard murder was a trend story, highlighting the prevalence of anti-gay hate crimes. But murders like Shepard's are extremely rare. In 1997, a relatively typical recent year, the FBI identified a total of eight hate-crime murders in the United States. The number that were gay-specific was even smaller. Most years, two or three occur at most. How common is a rape-murder like that of Dirkhising? In 1999 there were 46 rape-murders nationwide. If you focus not on the rape-murder aspect but on the fact that Jesse was a child, there were 1,449 murders of minors. There are no reliable statistics on how many of these

QUESTION: IS ONE HEINOUS MURDER MORE TRAGIC THAN ANOTHER?

MS. GIELINSKI WAS AN ATTRACTIVE COLLEGE STUDENT. IT APPEARS SHE WAS JUST IN THE WRONG PLACE AT THE WRONG TIME!

MR. SHEPARD WAS AN OPENLY GAY COLLEGE STUDENT. IT APPEARS HE WAS A VICTIM OF A HATE CRIME!

LOCAL MEDIA

NATIONAL MEDIA

Asay. © 1998 by Creators Syndicate, Inc. Reproduced by permission.

murders were committed by homosexuals, but let's generously say 5 percent. That's a paltry 72 cases. In other words, the murders of Shepard and Dirkhising are both extremely rare, and neither says much that can be generalized to the wider world. So why the obsession with Shepard and the indifference with regard to Dirkhising?

Some Deaths Are Worth More than Others

The answer is politics. The Shepard case was hyped for political reasons: to build support for inclusion of homosexuals in a federal hate-crimes law. The Dirkhising case was ignored for political reasons: squeamishness about reporting a story that could feed anti-gay prejudice, and the lack of any pending interest-group legislation to hang a story on. The same politics lies behind the media's tendency to extensively cover white "hate crimes" against blacks while ignoring black "non-hate crimes" against whites. What we are seeing, I fear, is a logical consequence of the culture that hate-crimes rhetoric promotes. Some deaths—if they affect a politically protected class—are worth more than others. Other deaths, those that do not fit a politically correct profile, are left to oblivion. The leading gay rights organization, the Human Rights Campaign—which has raised oodles of cash exploiting the horror of Shepard's murder—has said nothing whatsoever about the Dirkhising case. For the HRC, the murder of Jesse Dirkhising is off-message. Worse, there's a touch of embarrassment among some gays about the case, as if the actions of this depraved couple had some connection to the rest of gay America. Don't these squeamish people realize that, by helping to hush this up, they seem to confirm homophobic suspicions that this murder actually is typical of gays?

The irony is deepened by the fact that Jesse may well have been gay himself. He trusted his gay neighbors; he worked with one of them at a hair salon; his mother let him stay at his neighbors' place on weekends; it's even conceivable that at the beginning he went along with some part of their sexual game, as defense lawyers have argued. But he was also a child, in no position to consent to anything of this nature—a child who needed the support of his elders, not their monstrous betrayal. It's difficult for me to fully express my fury at this kind of behavior. For a young, impressionable boy like this to be used for sick sexual predation is an outrage to any homosexual who remembers being young or who has ever seen the need for guidance and support of a young gay soul. That some gay activists seem not to have experienced the same punch in the solar plexus that they felt when they heard of Shepard's murder is a sign of the moral damage that identity politics has already done. It has inured us to simple matters of good and evil. All that matters now, it seems, is us and them.

*"It's absurd . . . to deny the difference
between [hate crimes] and ordinary
crimes."*

Crimes Motivated by Bigotry
Deserve Special Punishment

Ellen Goodman

Because they appear to turn an emotion into a crime, it is
popular to criticize hate-crime laws, explains columnist
Ellen Goodman in the following viewpoint. Opponents of
such laws often argue that crimes provoked by bigotry
should be treated no differently than crimes rooted in other
motives. However, Goodman argues, hate crimes differ significantly from ordinary crimes. Hate crimes carry an extra
public dimension because they terrorize entire communities
and undermine societal pluralism. Consequently, bias-
motivated crimes deserve penalties beyond those reserved
for ordinary crimes, the author asserts.

As you read, consider the following questions:
1. According to Goodman, on what basis did white
   pharmacist Charles C. Apprendi appeal his hate-crime
   sentence to the Supreme Court?
2. What historical example does Goodman use to illustrate
   the difference between a hate crime and "ordinary
   vandalism"?
3. According to Brian Levin, quoted by the author, how do
   hate crimes affect society?

Ellen Goodman, "Hate Crimes Based on Bias and Bigotry," *Boston Globe*,
December 3, 1999. Copyright © 1999 by Globe Newspaper Company.
Reproduced by permission of Copyright Clearance Center, Inc.

It's too bad that we are stuck with the moniker "hate crimes." The label makes it sound as if it were a crime to hate. It's given opponents of hate crime laws a handle for all sorts of cliches: "Every crime is a hate crime." "Nobody commits a love crime."

Today it's become politically correct—in the true meaning of that phrase—to disparage laws that make it worse to commit a crime when the motive is bias. It's become popular to belittle the notion that society has an investment in upping the ante on such acts of bigotry.

Hate crimes are on the docket again because [in December 1999] the Supreme Court decided to hear the case of Charles C. Apprendi. [In 1994], Apprendi, a white pharmacist in Vineland, New Jersey, fired his rifle into the home of the only African-American family in his neighborhood. He told the police he wanted to give the family a message that they didn't belong.

Of course, by the time the trial came around, Apprendi denied that he was motivated by the color of their skin: brown. What set him off, he said, was the color of their door: purple. The judge, however, decided that the crime was racially motivated and so, under the New Jersey law on hate crimes, a 5- to 10-year sentence was kicked up to 12 years.

Now Apprendi has come to the Supreme Court demanding that a jury, not a judge, decide his motives.[1]

The New Jersey case is a relatively minor shot at the target of hate crime laws. But Apprendi's lawyers are trying to rein in the law. They are counting on the view that hate is too dicey an emotion, too elusive a motive.

This is what's happening to hate crime legislation: In the 1980s more than 40 states passed laws against crimes of bias, crimes committed against someone on the grounds of their religion or race.

Not a single hate crime law has passed since the [1998] dragging death of [black man] James Byrd Jr. Not a single existing law has been expanded to include homosexuality since the [1998] murder of [gay college student] Matthew Shepard. A Senate bill that would have accorded the modest

---

1. In 2000, the Supreme Court ruled that such cases had to be tried before a jury.

Biased Thought and Violence

Biased thought against a particular group has frequently erupted into violence. Throughout history, violence has often been used to prevent individuals from exercising their government-protected rights. In fact, the original function of the Ku Klux Klan, formed in Pulaski, Tennessee in 1866, was to intimidate and threaten black men who attempted to vote or run for political office. Klan members beat and lynched many would-be black voters and politicians before Congress forced the group to disband in 1871. The Klan has since been revived several times, continuing to intimidate and use violence against members of groups that it opposes, particularly blacks, but also Jews, Roman Catholics and immigrants.

The Klan's often violent activities prompted Congress to pass the first federal law banning hate crimes in 1968. The law, simply called Section 245 of Title 18 U.S.C. (U.S. Code), prohibited violence motivated by bias against a person on account of race, color, religion or national origin when that violence is meant to keep the victim from exercising a federally protected right.

Issues and Controversies On File, December 25, 1998.

---

federal hate-crime protection to sexual preference and gender was . . . rejected by Congress.

A crime is a crime is a crime, we are told. What difference does it make, opponents ask, if you attack a person as an individual or on account of his race, her religion, their sexual preference? What difference does it make if Matthew Shepard was brutally murdered because he was gay or because he was, say, short? What difference does it make if a hate crime penalty is added on to a murder conviction? Two life sentences?

Hate Crimes Are Different

Well, in fact, you cannot add on to a death sentence, and the families of murder victims do feel their pain equally, regardless of the killer's motives. But most hate crimes are not murder and it's absurd—disingenuous—to deny the difference between these and ordinary crimes.

There was, after all, a huge difference between Kristallnacht—the night the Nazis rampaged through Jewish homes and businesses—and ordinary vandalism. And there is enormous difference between shooting someone's house because of the color of his door and because of the color of his skin.

Hate crimes, bias crimes, are disproportionately crimes against people, not property. They are committed, the research tells us, by strangers, by groups, by "thrill seekers." They tend to escalate from a broken window to a broken bone.

But more than that they are, in Brian Levin's words, "a crime against community and a crime against a pluralistic society." A former police officer who is now a professor at California State University in San Bernardino, Levin has been studying hate crimes for 14 years and has come to believe that crimes motivated by bias "imprint on the rest of society a level of distrust. They're additional poison injected into society."

I don't deny that it can be hard to uncover someone's motive. Not everyone confesses or leaves graffiti on a sidewalk. We cannot read minds or punish people for their bigoted "feelings." But motive often plays a part in punishment and courts often wrestle with this problem of "why."

Today hate crime laws are often criticized as a kind of criminal affirmative action, "special protection" for "special classes of victims." In fact they apply to everyone and have since the first Supreme Court case upheld a hate crime law when a black man urged a crowd to assault a white passerby yelling, "There goes a white boy. Go get him."

So, it isn't a crime to hate. But when crime is based on bias or bigotry, when it's as directed as an act of terrorism against an entire group, it carries an extra and public dimension. That's when there—still—ought to be a law.

"If you . . . are viciously attacked during a robbery . . . , should the person who did this to you get less prison time because it was not an official 'hate crime'?"

Crimes Motivated by Bigotry Do Not Deserve Special Punishment

Nat Hentoff

Laws that impose harsher sentences on those who commit crimes motivated by hate are unfair to victims and perpetrators, argues columnist Nat Hentoff in the following viewpoint. Hentoff contends that all victims of the same type of crime, regardless of the reasons the crime was committed, deserve equal recompense. He maintains that hate-crimes laws are also unfair to perpetrators because they allow them to be tried twice—first in state courts and, if the punishment is deemed inadequate, then in federal courts; according to Hentoff, this provision of the law is in violation of the Fifth Amendment's prohibition against double jeopardy. Finally, he claims, in order to prove that perpetrators were motivated by hate, prosecutors are probing their backgrounds for suggestions of bigotry, a violation of Fourth Amendment privacy rights.

As you read, consider the following questions:
1. What criticism does Hentoff levy against the Schumer-Kennedy Hate Crimes Prevention Act?
2. What elements of a criminal's background are state prosecutors investigating in order to prove the perpetrator is bigoted, according to Hentoff?

Nat Hentoff, "The Case Against Hate-Crimes Laws," *Village Voice*, December 15, 1998. Copyright © 1998 by Nat Hentoff. Reproduced by permission.

S oon after the October 1998 murder of Matthew Shepard, hundreds of mourners held a vigil in Washington. Chanting "Now! Now! Now!" they demanded that Congress pass the Schumer-Kennedy hate-crimes legislation.

Also supporting the bill is House Democratic leader Richard Gephardt, who says the law is surely needed. And on October 19, 1998, Attorney General Janet Reno met with representatives of more than a dozen gay and lesbian groups and assured them she would renew her call for passage of hate-crimes legislation.

I have appeared on radio and television to debate various representatives of the ACLU [American Civil Liberties Union] and gay and lesbian groups about the value and ramifications of laws mandating *additional* prison terms for crimes designated as having been committed because of hatred of gays, lesbians, the disabled, blacks, Jews, Catholics, et al.

Unequal Sentencing

I start with a case: A young black man was injured so badly during a robbery that he was hospitalized. The perpetrator, a black man, received a prison sentence.

In another case, in the same city, a white man was assaulted by a black robber who yelled racial epithets during the attack. That victim was also hospitalized. Caught and convicted, this black criminal received a longer prison term than the black man who beat up the young black man.

The mother of the first victim asked an assistant district attorney why the man who attacked her son so viciously was sentenced to less prison time than the criminal who beat the white man.

She was told that the assault against the white man was, under law, a hate crime and therefore required additional punishment on top of the penalty for the assault itself.

"So," the mother said, "the harm done to my son counts for less than the harm done to the white man."

In a letter to *Newsday* (November 11, 1998), Michael Gorman, a lawyer and a New York City police lieutenant who supports hate-crimes laws, pointed out:

An antigay hate-crime assault will get much more attention from the district attorney's office and the police department.

. . . The criminal penalty often dictates the amount of effort detectives will put into a case, and hate crimes generally warrant more effort, both for the good of society at large and to protect the target victim and his or her identifiable group.

But if the "target victim" has been assaulted by someone bent *only* on robbery or because of a personal dispute—and if there is no evidence that the crime was fueled by bigotry—*that* criminal will get a lesser sentence because the actual criminal assault is not a "hate crime."

What, then, happens to "equal protection of the laws" as it concerns victims of violence?

If you, any of you, are viciously attacked during a robbery or during a "road rage" assault, should the person who did this to you get less prison time because it was not an official "hate crime"?

Violating the Fifth Amendment

Furthermore, if the Schumer-Kennedy Hate Crimes Prevention Act becomes law—and I'm reasonably sure it will be passed by the Congress and then signed by the president—there will be an increase in double jeopardy as initially prohibited by the Fifth Amendment to the Constitution:

"Nor shall any person be subject for the same offense to be twice put in jeopardy of life or limb."

The Schumer-Kennedy bill makes violence committed against anyone because of his or her gender, sexual orientation, or disability a federal crime. (The senators' staffs say that other categories of hate crime are covered by previous federal laws.)

This means—as David Harris, executive director of the American Jewish Committee, said in a letter to the *New York Times*—that there will be "the need for prosecution at the federal level if and when the local authorities fail to act or when state penalties are inadequate."

Despite the clear wording of the double-jeopardy clause of the Fifth Amendment, the courts have decided that it is lawful to try a person for the same crime in both the state and federal courts. (That has already happened to the police who beat Rodney King, as well as to Lemrick Nelson, for what he did during the Crown Heights riot.)

But it's worth emphasizing what Supreme Court Justice Hugo Black said, in dissent, in *Bartkus v. Illinois* (1959):

> The court apparently takes the position that a second trial for the same act is somehow less offensive [to the Fifth Amendment] if one of the trials is conducted by the federal government and the other by the state. *Looked at from the standpoint of the individual who is prosecuted, this notion is too subtle for me to grasp.* (Emphasis added.)

My argument against the effects of hate-crimes laws does recognize that the Supreme Court has unanimously declared that such legislation and the accompanying double-jeopardy possibilities are constitutional (*Wisconsin v. Mitchell*, 1993). It was a bizarre decision, but that's it.

An Arbitrary Distinction

The truth is, the distinction between a crime filled with personal hate and a crime filled with group hate is an essentially arbitrary one. It tells us nothing interesting about the psychological contours of the specific actor or his specific victim. It is a function primarily of politics, of special interest groups carving out particular protections for themselves, rather than a serious response to a serious criminal concern. In such an endeavor, hate-crime-law advocates cram an entire world of human motivations into an immutable, tiny box called hate, and hope to have solved a problem. But nothing has been solved; and some harm may even have been done.

In an attempt to repudiate a past that treated people differently because of the color of their skin, or their sex, or religion or sexual orientation, we may merely create a future that permanently treats people differently because of the color of their skin, or their sex, religion or sexual orientation. This notion of a hate crime, and the concept of hate that lies behind it, takes a psychological mystery and turns it into a facile political artifact. Rather than compounding this error and extending it even further, we should seriously consider repealing the concept altogether.

Andrew Sullivan, *New York Times*, September 26, 1999.

Why, then, continue the debate? Because it will be useful, when the Schumer-Kennedy bill becomes law, to know what's in store for the nation once the FBI is empowered to deal with alleged hate crimes under this new federalization of those crimes.

Violating the Fourth Amendment

Over-intrusive investigations have already taken place in various state prosecutions, such as Illinois (*People v. Lampkin*, 1983). Alleged perpetrators of these crimes have been probed with regard to their past associations, casual remarks, reading habits, and other presumable indications of bigotry. Some of these random invasions of Fourth Amendment privacy protections go back years.

For documentations of these Joe McCarthy–like abuses, see *Hate Crimes: Criminal Law and Identity Politics* (Oxford University Press) by NYU law professor James Jacobs and researcher Kimberly Potter. And white supremacist Tom Metzger advises callers to his telephone hot line to remain silent while committing a bias attack.

Periodical Bibliography

The following articles have been selected to supplement the diverse views presented in this chapter.

Paul Becker	"Hate Crimes on the Rise," *State Government News*, October 2001.
Chitra Divakaruni	"Being Dark-Skinned in a Dark Time: What Is It Like to Look 'Different' in America Today?" *Good Housekeeping*, January 2002.
Darryl Fears	"A Surge of Hate Crimes," *Washington Post National Weekly Edition*, December 2–6, 2002.
Bob Herbert	"Staring at Hatred," *New York Times*, February 28, 1999.
Jeffrey C. Isaac	"Responding to Hate," *Dissent*, Winter 2000.
Philip Jenkins	"A Vast White-Wing Conspiracy?" *Chronicles*, May 2000.
John Leo	"Not Fit to Print?" *U.S. News & World Report*, April 16, 2001.
Claude Lewis	"Violent Acts by One Don't Overshadow Good Acts by Most," *Philadelphia Inquirer*, July 16, 1999.
Robert Stacy McCain	"Hate Debate," *Insight on the News*, June 19, 2000.
Lowell Ponte	"The Secret Hate in 'Hate Crimes,'" *Ideas on Liberty*, February 2001.
Maria Purdy	"Hate Crime Horror Stories," *Teen*, March 2000.
Adam Pruzan	"What Is a Hate Crime?" *American Enterprise*, January 2000.
Ralph Reiland	"Horrors in the Courts," *American Enterprise*, March/April 1999.
Shashi Tharoor	"Letter from America," *Newsweek International*, October 29, 2001.
Tarynn M. Witten and A. Evan Eyler	"Hate Crimes and Violence Against the Transgendered," *Peace Review*, September 1999.

CHAPTER 2

What Motivates People to Hate?

Chapter Preface

Analysts have various theories on what causes people to join extremist groups and why some individuals in these groups eventually commit hate crimes. Some of the theories point to individual pathologies while others implicate social forces as the causes of hate.

Some experts believe that many people who engage in bias-motivated violence are mentally ill or emotionally unbalanced. While not all who suffer from mental illness turn to violence, mentally ill people who become involved in an extremist subculture are more likely to see violence as a justifiable moral choice. This may have been the case with Buford Furrow Jr., who killed a Filipino American postal worker and injured several people at a Jewish community center during a summer 1999 shooting spree in southern California. As analyst Chip Berlet explains, "Furrow came out of an apocalyptic neo-Nazi subculture that demonized Jews, people of color, and the government. The political/theological outlook sets the stage, but it is the mental illness that writes the script [when] someone pulls the trigger or commits other acts of violence." Berlet also points out, however, that even sane people in groups that demonize others can become so frustrated that "the barriers to violence are simply breeched by arguments that the violence prevents a greater moral harm." Therefore, he concludes, mental illness plays a part in some—but not all—hate crimes.

Other analysts maintain that certain social conditions— such as an economic upheaval or an apparent change in the balance of power between whites and minorities—boost hate crimes and hate group membership. This "environmental change" theory may help explain why young people raised in seemingly tolerant homes can become involved with hate groups. As *New York Times* columnist Bob Herbert reports, "Racist gangs . . . are having a field day recruiting [white] youngsters, often from suburbia, whose families are beleaguered financially and losing faith in their dream of a stable middle-class existence." Hate-group recruiters draw these youths in by telling them that they are "special" and that blacks and Jews are to blame for economic difficulties among middle-class whites, states Herbert. Although economic distress alone does not cause ethnic hatred, he explains, it does create vulnerability among troubled youths, making it easier to persuade them to vent their anger on minority scapegoats.

Emotional instability and socioeconomic distress are just two of the factors that might provoke people to act on their prejudices. The authors in the following chapter discuss these motivating factors as well as the roles that religious rhetoric and the Internet may play in fostering hatred.

"Entire nations have been incited by incendiary speech to exterminate whole categories of their fellow humans."

Religious Conservative Rhetoric Fosters Hatred

Sarah J. McCarthy

In the following viewpoint freelance writer Sarah J. Mc-Carthy argues that the ideas and rhetoric of religious conservatives create a climate in which hatred flourishes. For example, conservative claims that gay people are "abominations" and that abortion providers are "baby killers" can lead to justifications for perpetrating violence on homosexuals and physicians, she maintains. Conservatives who demonize entire groups of people are deservedly perceived as hate-inducing zealots, McCarthy concludes.

As you read, consider the following questions:
1. According to a poll cited by McCarthy, what percentage of Americans believes that the rhetoric of the anti-abortion movement increases the threat of violence against abortion clinics?
2. In the author's opinion, why do conservatives' denials about the potentially harmful effect of speech fall flat?
3. What has been the overall conservative reaction to abortion clinic terrorism, according to McCarthy?

Sarah J. McCarthy, "Fertile Ground for Terrorists?" *Humanist*, vol. 59, January 1999, p. 15. Copyright © 1999 by the American Humanist Association. Reproduced by permission.

Religious conservatives are angry at widespread accusations that their holy wars against gays and abortion doctors have created a climate that encourages violence. "The constant degrading of homosexuals is exacting a toll in blood," says *Newsweek* columnist Jonathan Alter—an assertion that conservative columnist Don Feder denounces as "bizarre." Does Alter actually think, asks Feder, that, if some "yahoo in the hinterlands" believes the religious institutions that declare homosexuality a disorder, he'll have "to go out and bash a queer"? Well, not exactly, Mr. Feder.

Those yahoos in the hinterlands who robbed, killed, and tied Matthew Shepard to a fence post may have been just as influenced by class envy, aimed at rich kids whose parents send them to prestigious schools—as Shepard's did—while the losers in life's lottery collect aluminum cans for a living or fish for catfish in the boondocks. Feder probably doesn't think it's bizarre when someone argues that class envy rhetoric, aimed at rich people or store owners, has exacted a toll in blood, at times leading to the incitement of armed robberies, burglaries, riots, lootings, rebellions, and even violent revolutions.

When conditions were right, entire nations have been incited by incendiary speech to exterminate whole categories of their fellow humans—for one reason or another. Every one of these mass-murder movements had intellectual or religious organizations that provided the justification for their brand of "purifying" their nation. Speech, as Feder knows, is a powerful thing. Why else would he write columns?

Conservative Denial

According to a *Newsweek* poll, six out of ten Americans believe the inflammatory rhetoric of the anti-abortion movement has led to a climate in which abortion clinics are more likely to be targeted for violence. A similar number think the government should be doing more to protect abortion clinics. Pat Buchanan, however, denies that his fellow social conservatives have played any part in fanning the flames. His denial comes as clinics are besieged with a flurry of shootings and bombings, threats of anthrax in the mail, and radical priests like the Reverend Donald Spitz of Pro-Life Virginia pronouncing the sniper who killed abortion provider Dr.

Barnett Slepian in Amherst, New York, "a hero."

What if there were a pro-choice website similar to the real anti-abortion website that encourages true believers to kill abortion doctors? One can only begin to imagine the hue and cry that would ensue if Buchanan or Feder were to discover that pro-choice proponents were encouraging the killing of anti-abortionists, with lines through the names of those already killed and the names of the living, their children, and addresses.

Britt. © 1998 by Copley News Service. Reprinted with permission.

Buchanan and other conservatives have written robust articles about the insidious dangers of rap music and Hollywood values that have led to cultural pollutants like promiscuity, drug use, and the rape and degradation of women. During his 1992 presidential campaign. Buchanan commented in a speech that the Los Angeles riots were the work of "a mob that came out of rock concerts where rap music celebrates raw lust and cop killing." How is the rhetoric about killing gays and abortion providers different?

If people were not influenced by words and ideas, there would be no point in having schools, churches, or advertisements. The more respected an institution, the more power of persuasion it holds over the actions of its followers. But to pound away at the idea that one group should be targeted as special sinners deserving of ridicule is not a good moral or strategic policy. To regularly proclaim a class of people as "abominations" is an insidious way to dehumanize and demonize.

Even the "respectable" social conservatives have chimed in, comparing gays to kleptomaniacs and alcoholics—mentally deranged folks who need help for their own good. Snipers who murder abortion providers are people they can sort of understand. Although a few conservatives have weakly condemned clinic terrorism, the overall reaction has been silence. They should, instead, offer constructive tactics that will lead to the need for fewer abortions.

If religious groups were to begin a campaign focusing on the sin of gluttony by spotlighting fat people, boycotting them from TV sitcoms, jeering at them, dehumanizing them, and demanding that companies take away their health insurance, it probably wouldn't be long before the death tolls for fat people began to rise.

Conservatives were incensed about the ads in the New York Senate race that helped defeat incumbent Alfonse D'Amato by portraying him as a supporter of clinic bombings because he voted on First Amendment grounds against a protection act that increased clinic security. Democratic political analyst Dick Morris responded that the anti-D'Amato ads were merely the flip side of tactics used by the anti-abortion movement to smear anyone who had reservations about banning late-term abortions. Gubernatorial candidate Christine Todd Whitman of New Jersey was portrayed by conservatives as a fan of late-term abortions because she wanted an exemption added to protect the mother's health. Other candidates were treated similarly.

In litmus-test politics and holy wars, truth is the first casualty. More effective than government force and political scare tactics are methods that convince, educate, and persuade. If social conservatives continue on their present-course—condemning people as "abominations" and "baby killers" and the like—they will continue to be condemned as big-government zealots who generate violence and hatred.

"[There is] a new campaign to paint conservative or traditional theological views as inherently hateful."

Religious Conservative Rhetoric Does Not Foster Hatred

Mark Tooley

The beliefs and ideas of religious conservatives do not incite hate, argues Mark Tooley in the following viewpoint. However, some liberal church leaders define hatred as any opposition to their political agenda concerning abortion, homosexuality, and other social issues, Tooley states. When religious traditionalists object to behaviors that they believe are immoral, for example, liberals claim that these objections lead to hate crimes against certain groups. In Tooley's opinion it is actually liberals who exhibit intolerance when they stigmatize conservative beliefs as inherently hateful. Tooley is a research associate at the Institute on Religion and Democracy in Washington, D.C.

As you read, consider the following questions:
1. According to Tooley, how would the religious left "cleanse" the allegedly hateful attitudes of conservatives?
2. What is hypocritical about liberal arguments for tolerance, in the author's view?
3. In Tooley's opinion, where does genuine hatred originate from?

S ome mainline Protestant church leaders are gearing up for campaigns against "hate." On the surface, it sounds like a worthy Christian endeavor. But read the not-so-fine print. "Hatred," by their new definition, includes any opposition to their political agenda regarding homosexuality, abortion, welfare reform, and affirmative action.

Opposition to any of these four is confirmation of hateful attitudes that must be cleansed through federal legislation or, at the very least, sensitivity indoctrination by the religious left's enlightened few. Recent publications from the United Methodist and Presbyterian (U.S.A.) Churches highlight the new campaign to paint conservative or traditional theological views as inherently hateful.

The Rhetoric of the Religious Left

A whole [1999] issue of the United Methodist Women's magazine, *Reponse*, was devoted to supposedly growing currents of American "hate" and the proper Christian response to it. Oddly, but not surprisingly, one of the writers was the head of the Unitarian Universalist Association's Washington office, Meg Riley, a prominent "gay" and pro-abortion activist.

Riley was especially distressed by the testimonies of former homosexuals and by the Christian groups that helped them become celibate or heterosexual. She asks: "Why not assume [they] are stating their own truth, then ask what that has to do with their campaign to deny others' right to speak a different truth—the truth of happy, fulfilled, faithful, nonheterosexual lives?"

Ministries to transform homosexuals are merely a Trojan Horse to disenfranchise homosexuals, she remarks. Similarly, welfare reform laws, although touted as compassionate, are really intended to stigmatize the poor as "lazy, dishonest, and passive." The Promise Keepers movement is just camouflage for efforts to subordinate women to their husbands. And the pro-life movement likewise aims to deprive women of their equality. Riley conspiratorially surmises that "right-wing" groups enlist black conservatives as marionettes to mouth their opposition to affirmative action laws.

Tragically, according to Riley, the media are unable to look behind the trickery of conservatives who are manipulating "confessional melodrama" to paste happy faces on their oppressive causes. (Riley is really upset that traditionalists have caught on to the modern media technique of advocating a cause through storytelling instead of abstract argument.)

Liberal Intolerance

In a similarly histrionic vein, Mab Segrest of North Carolinians Against Racist and Religious Violence alleged in the Methodist magazine that "within Christianity, church fiat is the equivalent of [the] pistols" employed by Matthew Shepard's killers.[1] Not content to condemn the United Methodist Church, she lashed out at Joseph Cardinal Ratzinger, prefect of the Congregation for the Doctrine of the Faith, for opposing civil legislation that would codify protection of "sexual orientation." Ratzinger wants to protect the definition of "genuine families" from nontraditional alternatives, Segrest fumed.

Opposition to full sexual freedom is an emblem of burgeoning hate, liberal church leaders are increasingly claiming. The Presbyterian Church's *Church and Society* magazine late [in 1999] focused on hatred. In her introduction, the editor even surmised that the "facile platitude, 'hate the sin, not the sinner,' actually begets hate-motivated violence against the homosexual community." By her logic, opposition to any behavior on moral grounds inevitably leads to church-sanctioned violence against its practitioners. The only solution, it would seem, is unilateral moral disarmament and complete moral relativism.

Neither she nor the other writers in her magazine acknowledged the hypocrisy of their argument for tolerance, as they intolerantly berate conservatives for daring to voice their disagreement with liberal conventional wisdom on social relations.

Also writing in the Presbyterian magazine was an activist with the Religious Coalition for Reproductive Choice, who discerned that the "root of the anti-abortion fever is patriarchy" which suggests that "men are superior to women." Re-

1. In 1998 Shepard, a homosexual college student, died after being beaten and pistol-whipped by two men he had met in a Wyoming bar.

ducing women to second-class citizens eases the guilt when violent acts are committed, he concluded. Himself a United Methodist minister, he laments the "homophobia" of his own denomination for not tolerating same-sex ceremonies.

Religious Conservative Views

What kind of America *do* religious conservatives believe in? It is a nation of safe streets, strong families, schools that work, and marriages that stay together, one with a smaller government, lower taxes, and civil rights for all. Most religious conservatives do not countenance discrimination—or special rights—for anyone. Our faith is simple, and our agenda is direct.

For either political party to attack persons holding these views as "fanatics," "extremists," or worse violates a basic American spirit of fairness. More than that, it runs counter to all we are as a nation and all we aspire to be as a people.

Ralph Reed, *USA Today Magazine*, July 1997.

A minister from the homosexual Universal Fellowship of Metropolitan Community Churches was another writer for *Church and Society* who predictably likened opposition to homosexuality to racism. The real issue, he insisted, is more than just world debt, racism, sexism, homophobia, ethnonationalism, ableism, and ageism, as he recited the full litany of politically correct bugaboos. The real cause for opposition to the "inclusion" of all people is simply fear.

He concluded by quoting South African Anglican prelate Desmond Tutu: "We can be human only together [as] lesbian, gay, bisexual, transgendered, and heterosexual Christians." (Notice the ever-lengthening list of sexual predilections that are included under the mantra of "inclusiveness," where "relationship" has replaced marriage as the Christian prerequisite for sexual relations.)

The Real Cause of Hatred

The religious left's crusade to stigmatize traditional and conservative beliefs as inherently hateful is not only a smear, it is intellectually sloppy. Revisionist church leaders are perhaps so overconfident in their ultimate victory in the culture wars that they believe sound reasoning is not required to prevail. Or, trapped in their own postmodernist vortex, they have ceased to recognize the difference between logic and emotional outbursts.

Either way, religious traditionalists need to be able to explain that the "facile platitude" of "hate the sin, love the sinner," is actually neither. It is rather a profound summary of the Gospel's approach to all of us who violate God's standards and stand in need of His grace.

And defenders of historic Christian beliefs must also point out that genuine hatred originated neither with Christianity nor with the "patriarchy." It flows from the sinful nature to which all persons are captive, and for which the only full remedy is Jesus Christ.

United Methodist and Presbyterian magazines should be able to understand.

"[Gay bashers] attempt to destroy in others the homosexuality they see and despise in themselves."

Homophobia Fosters Hatred

Mubarak Dahir

Males who commit antigay violence are often insecure about their own masculinity and assault others to destroy the homosexuality that they fear in themselves, explains Mubarak Dahir in the following viewpoint. The excessive brutality that is seen in many antigay hate crimes suggests that perpetrators may be deeply conflicted about their own sexuality. Some gay bashers, however, could be responding to peer pressure to denigrate homosexuality rather than personal fears about their own sexual orientation, notes Dahir. Yet each kind of hatred—personal or social—is rooted in homophobia, he reports. Dahir is a contributing writer to the *Advocate*, a biweekly newsmagazine focusing on issues of importance to the gay community.

As you read, consider the following questions:
1. According to Dahir, what is "projective identification"?
2. What is the "gay panic" defense, according to the author?
3. What psychological traits do many gay bashers share in common, according to this viewpoint?

Mubarak Dahir, "The Urge to Kill," *Advocate*, September 12, 2000, pp. 33–36.

On the evening of July 3, Arthur "J.R." Warren decided to drop in on some friends in his hometown of Grant Town, W. Va. He wasn't seen alive again.

Authorities say Warren, a gay 26-year-old African-American with a learning disability, got into an argument with his friends, two teenage cousins. The boys, David Parker and Jared Wilson, kicked Warren with steel-toed shoes, officials say. Although bloodied, Warren was still alive. The boys then reportedly put him into their Camaro, where Warren climbed over the backseat and asked to be taken home. The cousins are accused of instead attempting to cover up the beating by throwing Warren out of the car and then driving the car over his body four times. Only a frightened 15-year-old boy's eyewitness account kept police from calling the incident a hit-and-run accident.

What prompted a crime of such brutality among friends? According to court documents, Parker argued with Warren over "a rumor that had circulated." The rumor, according to press reports, was Warren's claim that he had had a sexual relationship with one or both of the boys. His death appears to be their attempt to silence him about it.

Warren's death is hardly the only attack in which suspects or convicted killers were reported to have had some kind of gay history. This has been the case in many of the well-publicized assaults on gay men in the past several years. Also, the violence of antigay attacks—which far outstrips the brutality of other bias crimes—shows just how personal the motivation is for such crimes. Bashers are not only trying to kill the victim; they are, in some sense, trying to kill their own gay side and reassure themselves and their friends about their own masculinity. The attempt to destroy in others the homosexuality they see and despise in themselves has been dubbed "projective identification" by psychologists.

"The level of hatred these men have for themselves can be staggering," says Arthur Ciaramicoli, a clinical psychologist on faculty at Harvard Medical School. "They take what they don't want to see and can't accept in their own self-image and project it onto someone else. Then they can hate it because they've divorced it from who they are. Essentially, they're beating out in others what they are scared of in themselves."

The Underlying Connection

Indeed, in a number of the most recent high-profile attacks, there has been an underlying gay connection in the suspect's life. Often these facts emerge after the first crush of media attention and thereby go unnoticed. For example, attorneys for Aaron McKinney, one of two men to plead guilty in the [1998] death of Matthew Shepard, argued during his trial that their client had been left angry and confused by a consensual sexual experience with a male cousin. There are several other assaults in which the accused assailant's own gay past has been revealed.

• Pvt. Justin Fisher goaded Pvt. Calvin Glover to take a bat to Pfc. Barry Winchell's skull as he lay sleeping in a cot. Earlier in their friendship Fisher had fondled Winchell's feet, and it was Fisher who initially took Winchell to the Connection, Nashville's largest gay bar. It was a place Fisher repeatedly frequented, flirting and making out with drag queens.

• In Alabama, 26-year-old skinhead Steve Mullins was convicted of killing Billy Jack Gaither. During the trial of Mullins's codefendant, Charles Butler Jr., witnesses testified that Mullins had previously engaged in sex with other men.

• In the notorious *Jenny Jones* case, Jonathan Schmitz was convicted of having killed Scott Amedure days after Amedure admitted during a taping of Jones's show that he had a crush on Schmitz. However, Amedure's mother said her son told her after the taping that he had had sex with Schmitz.

• Matthew Williams, who is accused with his brother Tyler of killing a gay couple in their home near Redding, Calif. [in 1999], had an intense—but platonic—romance with a man who subsequently came out as gay.

The "Gay Panic" Defense

Ironically enough, the idea that the violence of gay bashers may be the result of emotional turmoil has been a key part of their legal strategies. The so-called "gay panic" defense argues that the attacker was justified in turning to violence because of a sexual advance made by the victim. That the reaction is far out of proportion to any rational response underscores the basher's own discomfort and insecurity regarding gay sexuality.

But sometimes there is no prior sexual link between victim and perpetrator. In those instances the catalyst for the attack seems even harder to find.

Many men feel conflicted about sexual desires they have for other men, says Jack Levin, a criminologist who is director of Northeastern University's Brudnick Center on Violence and author of the book *Hate Crimes*. Yet most men struggling with their feelings of homosexuality do not respond with violence against gays. Someone who does, says Levin, "is a person for whom the idea of his own sexuality is so unacceptable that the mere presence of a gay person is threatening." To this type of person, he says, the thought of his sexual desires "is an overwhelming threat to his masculinity and self-image."

Self-Hatred and Bullying

Jenna Ard, a 20-year-old student at Loyola University in New Orleans, says she became a bully after she was teased in the fourth grade by someone who thought she was gay. After that, Ard says, she transformed herself from a soccer-playing tomboy into a sorority girl and self-described "hostess of homophobia": "I used words like 'dykey' and 'fag' to describe kids who seemed even the slightest bit [gay], and my friends laughed every time I did it."

And Ron Deutsch, 39, of Los Angeles says that when his classmates started to pick up on the fact that he might be gay, he masked his sexual orientation by bullying another boy on the school bus every day. "I really verbally abused him a lot, when I knew that I was wrestling with my own sexuality and that I was sort of attracted to him," Deutsch says. "When you are being oppressed, it is easy to become the oppressor."

David Kirby, *Advocate*, July 3, 2001.

Such an individual, agrees Ciaramicoli, "is in the extreme situation where his sense of self cannot exist under those conditions. He feels homosexual feelings mean he cannot be loved, tolerated, or accepted in his world."

Those who lash out in violence as a result of projective identification, says Ciaramicoli, tend to share several psychological traits. First, perpetrators are uniformly men and are very young, most often in their teens or 20s. "That's when anxiety about masculinity is at the forefront," he says. Bashers are also likely to come from environments in which they "are taught to idealize aggression and violence as power," says Ciaramicoli, most commonly from "an aggressive father or other male figures."

Distinct Characteristics of Anti-Gay Crimes

One key component that distinguishes gay bashing from other hate crimes is that "it's not rooted in economic fears," says Levin. Trace the roots of racism and anti-Semitism, he says, and you will find economic motivation behind the hatred. "You can almost predict those who attack Jews or African-Americans or Latinos are those who are in—or feel they are in—direct economic competition and feel frightened and threatened by that. But gay bashers can come from any economic class."

Sheer brutality is another horrifyingly distinct characteristic of these crimes, adds Clarence Patton, director of public advocacy at the New York City Gay and Lesbian Anti-Violence Project. "Bias crimes committed against gays tend to be more physical than those committed against other targeted groups," says Patton, who says his organization is "not surprised when we discover cases where the perpetrators are torn by their own sexual issues."

There are even certain "red flags" that antiviolence experts have come to recognize as tip-offs that a case may carry a personal element, says Patton. Foremost among them is what is known as "overkill"—multiple stabbings, for example, or extreme mutilation of the victim's body, especially sex organs. Gaither not only had his throat cut; he was beaten with an ax handle and then set atop a pile of burning tires. Warren was run over four times. Winchell was attacked so viciously that his brains oozed out of his left ear.

Peer Pressure and Other Factors

Not everyone agrees with the theory of projective identification, arguing that it may not be self-hatred that motivates bashers but rather a more complicated mix of social factors, including fear of what peers think of them. Gregory Herek, a professor of psychology at the University of California,

Davis, and an expert on hate crimes, warns that researchers are only beginning to understand antigay violence and come up with explanations for it. "It's too early for sweeping generalizations," he says. "Sexual identity is very complex and little understood."

In fact, says Herek, studies of attacks committed by two or more bashers "show these guys are not particularly antigay. Their motivation is often more to avoid social rejection by their group. So it's a mistake to assume all antigay violence is based on homophobia."

While Herek concurs that there "is clearly a pattern of some perpetrators having sexual encounters with men," he cautions against using any single theory to explain gay bashing. He believes social conditions may be just as responsible for stoking violence as projective identification.

"In American society, being 'a man' is often a difficult undertaking. It's more defined by what you are not supposed to be than what you are supposed to be," he explains. "But one thing is clear: You're not supposed to be a sissy or a queer. That social pressure can have a huge impact on men who have sex with men and then bash gays. As much as what's going on inside his head, he may be trying to prove to other guys he's not a queer."

Armand Cerbone, former chairman of the Committee on Lesbian, Gay, and Bisexual Concerns of the American Psychological Association, agrees that one of the most important influences on gay bashers who exhibit gay tendencies is the powerful force of peer pressure: "You have to take both things into account—the environment of sexual orientation prejudice and an individual's personal demons." Young men struggling with their own sexuality "are particularly susceptible to peer pressure," he notes.

Whether it's personal hatred, social hatred, or a combination of both that leads these men to violence, "in some respects it's a rose by any other name," argues Cerbone. "It's that part of society that still has a deep-seated hatred for gays that teaches them their self-loathing."

4

"Hate groups operate along the fringe of our capitalist society, preying on the frustration it engenders."

The Inequality Rooted in Capitalism Fosters Hatred

David Tyler

Several factors are contributing to the development of hate groups in the United States, writes *New Unionist* columnist David Tyler in the following viewpoint. Poverty, income inequality, and a lack of education can make white youths more receptive to arguments that minorities are taking employment opportunities away from whites. Furthermore, Tyler explains, a growing number of youths are being sent to prison, where they are exposed to hate-group ideologies. All of these factors are rooted in capitalism, which exploits the average worker. As companies downsize and use more overseas labor to increase their profits, U.S. workers lose jobs and become increasingly frustrated. Hate groups take advantage of this frustration to expand their ranks, Tyler maintains.

As you read, consider the following questions:

1. According to Tyler, what percentage of households own 85 percent of the nation's wealth?
2. What facilities are prime areas targeted by hate-group recruiters, according to the author?
3. In Tyler's opinion, what is the only way to abolish hatemongering by hate groups?

S ince the Littleton massacre[1] there has been much written about hate speech on the Internet. Both of the young assassins in that event were avid fans of the Web sites of U.S. hate groups. These groups also peddle up to 50,000 recordings of white racist rock 'n roll to the younger generation each year.

Groups such as the neo-Nazi National Alliance and Hammerskin Nation, as well as the World Church of the Creator, another neo-Nazi outfit that spawned a midwestern shooting spree by associate Benjamin Smith, are gaining followings among the lower working class.

Why are so many young white people embracing organized hate today? An article in the "Intelligence Report" of the Southern Poverty Law Center gives a list of eight sets of statistics that lend insight into this problem.

Contributing Causes

First, according to this report, income inequality is now at its highest level since the Great Depression. 20% of U.S. households own 85% of the nation's wealth. Resentment on the part of those left out of the "prosperity" sets in. The hate groups claim that the Jews own more than their share of the pie and blame blacks for moving up at the expense of whites. These claims can often impress youth, even though they are factually baseless.

A second contributing factor is the rise of child poverty. Between 1973 and 1994 the number of children living in poverty doubled. At the same time families headed by a high school dropout saw their median income cut in half. Those with a high school diploma were cut by a third. Resentment over their harsh underprivileged existence by those concerned escalates, and the hate groups offer a channel for expressing those frustrations.

Lack of education is thus an interrelated factor. People 16–24 with only a high school education suffer from unemployment at twice the rate of college graduates, while the level for high school dropouts is five times that of college

---

1. a reference to the April 1999 school shootings at Columbine High School in Littleton, Colorado

grads. The Jewish conspiracy myth and the attack on blacks for stealing jobs from white youths can be used to lure in the less educated angry over lessened opportunities.

Youth-Related Factors

A fourth related factor is the dramatic decrease in real wages for younger persons. Workers between 20 and 29 have had their wages fall by 22% in the last 25 years. This leads to an increase in crime for the age group. According to the U.S. National Bureau of Economic Research, a 20% drop in wages translates into a 12–18% increase in crime. And prisons and juvenile detention facilities are prime areas targeted by hate groups for recruitment.

Juvenile arrests for violent crimes are up, and this is the fifth factor. While juveniles make up only 7% of the population their arrests for violent crimes increased by 79% between 1987 and 1994. Since 1994 the levels have declined but are still way above the levels of the 1980s. Once again, prison means exposure to the tactics of hate groups.

White Male Entitlement

For University of Colorado sociologist Abby Ferber, it all comes down to entitlement. Many white men, said Ferber, are raised with the belief that they are entitled to economic success, social leadership and personal happiness. And when they miss the mark in some or all of those areas, their frustration may fester into murderous rage, said Ferber, author of the 1998 book, *White Man Falling: Race, Gender and White Supremacy.*

"What's really troubling is that these men have so many historical references for their beliefs," said Ferber. "If you go back and look at the Founding Fathers, they were talking about the rights of white men. This started as a nation concerned with the property and personal rights of white males. So now, when white men feel that their entitlement to those rights is under attack, they have a tremendous sense of failure."

William R. Macklin, *Philadelphia Inquirer*, August 16, 1999.

The sixth factor is that young offenders are more likely to go to prison than previously. In 1972, 45% of youths arrested for crimes were released. That number has now been reduced by half in the "tough on crime" atmosphere engineered by right-wing politicians. There again young people are exposed to prison gangs which sport racist hate-group ideologies.

A seventh reason is that America's white majority is on the ebb, with the Hispanic population projected to grow to 25% of the population by the year 2050, blacks standing pat as a percentage of population, and Asians doubling in number by that year. Hate groups can thus play on demographics and portray the white race as beleaguered on all sides and losing a grip on "their" nation.

Separatist longings, not only among white youth but on the part of colored youths as well, round out the list as the eighth factor. Increasingly, separatist views are being held by young people who do not remember the society of pre–civil rights America.

In one survey 50.3% of youths either strongly agreed with or somewhat agreed with the statement, "It's okay if races are basically separate from one another as long as everyone has equal opportunities." The need for integration is lost on many poor or undereducated whites, and this provides fertile ground for racist hate-group propaganda.

The Globalized Capitalist Market

Of course, unmentioned in the Intelligence Report piece is that most of these factors are due to the globalized capitalist market and its ongoing struggle against the average worker. A host of interrelated ills has cropped up as big money cuts costs of production, downsizes and shifts more and more production overseas in order to increase profits. And these trends are going to continue as they follow the economic laws that govern capitalist production.

No matter how the debate regarding the globalized market is shaped, one thing is clear: labor costs must be kept to a minimum in order to realize maximum profit, and maximizing profit is the only way to remain competitive—that is, remain in business.

Hate groups operate along the fringe of our capitalist society, preying on the frustration it engenders. Until we alter the form of production we have now by making it democratically controlled and centered on human needs instead of profits, the present situation is going to repeat itself over and over. Hate groups will seek to take advantage just as they did in Hitler's Germany, Franco's Spain, Mussolini's Italy and dozens of other fascist governments.

The only way to abolish such hatemongering is to abolish the present system, the failure of which creates the conditions the hatemongers exploit.

"Without an alternative to the fantasies of white nationalism, we face an abyss of mayhem and murder."

White Nationalism Fosters Hatred

Leonard Zeskind

Hate groups such as the World Church of the Creator believe that the white race is endangered by Jews and minorities and are calling for a "racial holy war," explains Leonard Zeskind in the following viewpoint. Although many hate groups are small and cultish, their beliefs about racial purity are shared by a more widely based white nationalist movement—a group that includes skinheads, survivalists, militia members, and neo-Confederates, maintains Zeskind. Until Americans willingly identify themselves as a multiracial people, violence provoked by white nationalist values will remain a threat. Zeskind is president of the Institute for Research and Education on Human Rights in Kansas City, Missouri.

As you read, consider the following questions:
1. How does Matt Hale, quoted by the author, define the ideology of the World Church of the Creator?
2. According to Zeskind, what plight do all white nationalists believe they share in common?
3. What is Zeskind's response to the claim that hate crimes are fueled by economic distress?

Leonard Zeskind, "This Killer Didn't Just Blindly Hate: He Hated with a Vision," *Los Angeles Times*, July 7, 1999, p. B7. Copyright © 1999 by Leonard Zeskind. Reproduced by permission.

Once again [in July 1999] our country is horrified by the specter of Yugo-like murder.[1] This time, a 21-year-old university student, Benjamin Smith, allegedly killed two and wounded nine others in a three-day shooting spree through Illinois and Indiana that ended with him taking his own life.

As with the [April 1999] massacre at Columbine High School in Littleton, Colo., the perpetrator was a young, reasonably intelligent, white male from a comfortable suburban address. Also as with the mindless dragging death of James Byrd Jr. in Texas [in June 1998] and the fear-filled fence-post murder of Matthew Shepard in Wyoming [in October 1998], the motivation appears to be racism and bigotry. This is not blind hatred in the Heartland, however, but hate with a vision.

Racial Holy War

Smith was a dedicated cadre, selflessly devoting himself to a relatively small outfit calling itself the World Church of the Creator, led by a recent law school graduate, Matt Hale. The group cultivates an almost Nietzschean image of itself as the saviors of a "white race" imperiled by a "Jewish occupation government" and a "mud" flood of non-white peoples.

By the Creators' account, Christianity disarms whites with its "sickly" Jewish creed. On the other hand, Creativity—as Hale calls his ideology—is a "racial religion that embodies the best values of genetics, biology . . ." ad nauseam. Its first aim, claims the propaganda, is "a revolution of values." Church strategy calls for polarizing white people and driving all others out of the country. RAHOWA, or Racial Holy War, is the battle cry.

This "religion" has led to violence more than once. In all probability, it will do so again in the future. At first glance, it is a vision perverse, almost pornographic. Certainly the Creators' cultish commitment to Matt Hale's *fuhrer*-ship will confine it to the basement, even of the brown-shirt crowd. And its antipathy to any form of Christianity guarantees it will fail among the God, guts and guns set. Similarly, periodic outbursts of violence by Creativity's followers are sure to embarrass even those like David Duke, who share

1. a reference to the violent ethnic conflicts in Yugoslavia during the 1990s

Old Hatreds and New Rhetoric

Hate groups are refocusing their energies. They are worried that they can never convince the majority of white Americans to join them in their netherworld. While many whites may share their prejudices, very few are willing to act on them by openly carrying a Klan calling card or an Uzi. This situation demands a new strategy that combines old hatreds with new rhetoric. White supremacists desperately need to reinvigorate their movement with new recruits by manipulating white fears into action.

White fears of change or difference are exploited by hate groups. At the same time, they are expanding their targets of hate. They have adopted not only homophobia as a prominent part of their new agenda, but are forcefully anti-abortion, pro-family values, and pro-American, in addition to their traditional racist and anti-Semitic beliefs. This broadening of issues and the use of conservative buzzwords have attracted the attention of whites who may not consider themselves racist, but do consider themselves patriotic Americans concerned about the moral decay of "their" country.

Loretta Ross, *Public Eye*, 1995.

their belief in a "genetic" basis for white supremacy but aim at the more mainstream goal of electing themselves to office.

White Nationalism

But closer examination reveals that the Church of the Creators' underlying thesis, the yen for a "racially pure" country, is shared by a more broadly based white nationalist movement. Once the province of old-style Klansmen and neo-Nazis, this white nationalism now comes in many guises: White power skinheads rocking out to *oi* and death metal music. Army of God sympathizers hiding bombers in the Tennessee mountains. Survivalists preparing for civil unrest (read race war) alongside militia-men defending against a United Nations invasion. Neo-confederates resurrecting the Lost Cause and white-citizen-council types nipping at the edges of the Republican Party. All see themselves pressed between an internationalist elite and the multicultural masses. One wants to sell their jobs to Mexico, while the other swamps their supposed majority culture. Many find themselves in a mythology that combines the Founding Fathers, the Constitution and the Bible and bestows the full rights of citizenship only to white people.

White supremacists have taken a long march from the margins to the mainstream, like a guerilla army slowly encircling the cities. After 20 years of torchlight rallies, preaching, radio broadcasts and grass-roots organizing, they have built a distinctive constituency and counterculture institutions. But this isn't the white supremacy of Anglo-American slavery and genocide or Jim Crow segregation. This is a white nationalism for the future, opposed to the New World Order.

Some of my colleagues claim this blindingly white vision is created out of the fears of economic distress. Declining wages and bleak working-class prospects, they say, create a cycle of scapegoating and violence. But the incident involving Benjamin Smith demonstrates just the opposite. No economic angst here. He was solidly middle class, and his prospects were good. But there was a crisis nonetheless. It is a crisis of identity, a question of who we Americans are. Smith found himself barreling down a highway of hate, shooting innocents who did not belong in his Aryan world.

On the other hand, we are zooming into the future, without a firmly held collective vision of ourselves as a multiracial people. Without an alternative to the fantasies of white nationalism, we face an abyss of mayhem and murder.

"White sheets and burning crosses have given way to Web servers and URLs, to Aryan chat rooms, and electronic archives of paranoid propaganda."

White Supremacist Websites Foster Hatred

Richard Firstman

In the following viewpoint Richard Firstman discusses the development and impact of online hate groups, which have proliferated in the past few years. According to Firstman, a growing number of hate crimes are being committed by people who are influenced by information posted on the Internet. Several recent bias-motivated murders, for example, were perpetrated by young men who admit that their bigoted views were shaped or reinforced by hate sites. In addition, Firstman notes, established white supremacist leaders are using the Internet as a tool to recruit young people for their cause. Firstman, a New York–based writer, is coauthor of *The Death of Innocents.*

As you read, consider the following questions:
1. According to the author, how many hate sites existed in 1995? How many exist today?
2. How does the World Church of the Creator website attempt to appeal to young children, according to Firstman?
3. Which organizations have emerged to counter the influence of online hate groups, according to the author?

Richard Firstman, "Hate in Online America," *Family PC*, vol. 8, May 2001, p. 82.

[I~~n 1995]~~ there was one Web site espousing neo-Nazi views. Today there are more than 2,800, and their highly charged rhetoric is believed to be responsible for a number of high-profile crimes against non-Whites, gays, and Jews.

The announcement from the FBI [in the fall of 2000] seemed almost anticlimactic. After a two-year investigation, agents in San Diego had arrested 25-year-old Alex Curtis for painting anti-Semitic graffiti on two synagogues and harassing several local officials with hate-filled leaflets and stickers. But while the crimes alleged were detestable, surely unsettling to the victims, they were almost petty given Curtis's recent activities.

A Rising Star

By the time of his arrest, Curtis had emerged as a rising star of the new wave of organized racism in America. The archetype of the seething young ethnic anarchist for the Information Age, he operated a prolific Web site—whiteracist.com—and published a newsletter called the *Nationalist Observer*. By phone from the bedroom of his parents' home in a suburb of San Diego, complete with the requisite framed portrait of Adolf Hitler, he offered a "Weekly Racist Message," also available in both Real Audio and text on his Web site. Though Curtis is in jail awaiting trial, his Web site still boasts "the world's largest racist link page"—nearly 200 sites in all, many with abundant archives of hate-mongering material and links of their own.[1]

"We advocate complete racial separation," Curtis declares portentously through RealPlayer before opening the spigot on his virulent anti-Semitic, anti-Black, anti-authority rhetoric. "We repudiate the U.S. government and its programs to murder the pure races of mankind. We condemn all law enforcement and elections."

Curtis's racial fury has been many years in the making. When he was 17, he wrote in a diary that was later confiscated by police. "I plan to make it my life's goal to rid the Earth of the unwanted un-Aryan elements, by whatever

---

1. In June 2001 Alex Curtis was convicted on hate-crimes charges and sentenced to three years in prison.

means necessary and possible." According to an autobiography he e-mailed to subscribers [in 2000], Curtis came to this decision after becoming a "self-educated racist" at 13, starting a one-man Ku Klux Klan chapter in his hometown of Lemon Grove, Calif., and being arrested for vandalizing his high school with swastikas and racial epithets.

After graduation, he spent his time flooding San Diego with hate literature, some of which featured a police insignia and asked citizens to "help fight non-White crime."

In the years following what he calls these "small-time terrorist acts"—for which he was sentenced to probation and community service—Curtis began to think bigger. In 1997, he discovered the Internet, and began spreading his toxic gospel to a potential audience of millions, arguably becoming the most incendiary voice in the White-supremacy subculture. Curtis openly discussed assassination and filled his Web site with strategies for "lone wolves"—radical racists who act alone or in small groups so as not to jeopardize the larger movement—to target Jews, Blacks, and federal government officials.

But if Curtis's malevolence is boundless and his propaganda machine high-tech, his arrest in November [2000] seemed almost a throwback to his days as a decidedly low-tech local nuisance. Besides the graffiti charge, Curtis and three others were accused of harassing a Jewish congressman, the Hispanic mayor of the suburb of La Mesa, the head of the San Diego office of the Anti-Defamation League (ADL), and a local civil rights official.

The arrest took Curtis away from his computer, but his alleged crimes were not the sort that most concern law enforcement and civil rights officials. What they worry about is the ability of Curtis and other online hatemongers to inspire potential lone wolves. There are indications that some are hearing the call.

The Internet Connection

While federal statistics on reported hate crimes nationwide over the last decade have remained steady at about 8,000 a year, there has been a rise in the number of crimes committed by people whose views were either shaped or reinforced by what they found on the Internet. This comes at a time when the number of hate sites has gone from one, Stormfront.org, in 1995 to some 2,800 today.

"There is at least a tacit connection" asserts Rick Eaton, a senior researcher at the Simon Wiesenthal Center in Los Angeles and one of a growing number of investigators and advocates at the forefront of what has become a complex international legal and moral struggle with online hate.

When two California brothers, Matthew, 31, and Tyler Williams, 29, were arrested for the 1999 murders of a gay couple near Sacramento and suspected in the fire bombings of three synagogues, the FBI found evidence that the Williamses came to their extreme bigotry through the Internet. The brothers were not members of any racist group, but according to friends, the older Williams had become enraptured by what he found on the Internet and "turned bit by bit into what he became" in the words of one. Besides finding stacks of printouts from hate Web sites, the FBI agents discovered that phone calls had been made from the Williamses' house to two Web proprietors. Alex Curtis was one of them.

The other was Matt Hale. A . . . law school graduate from Illinois, Hale is the self-styled "Pontifex Maximus" of the World Church of the Creator, another major hate organization prominent on the Web.

"Reverend" Hale, as he calls himself, is perhaps best known for his association with one of the most infamous hate crimes in recent years. On July 2, 1999, as Hale announced that the Illinois bar had for a second time found him morally unfit to hold a license to practice law, his 21-year-old protege, Ben Smith, began a three-day, two-state shooting spree. By the time Smith was finished, a Black man and a Korean student were dead and six Orthodox Jews were injured. A doctor's son who had once been an A student with Jewish friends and an Asian-American girlfriend, Smith had told a documentarian that he'd had a racial awakening in his late teens, but that "it wasn't until I got on the Net that it all came together."

About to be captured on the Fourth of July 1999, Smith ended his rampage by turning his gun around and firing one last time. It was the final act of a would-be martyr whom Hale likes to believe went out in a blaze of glory. Hale credits Smith's weekend of violence with raising the profile of their cause and bringing scores of new visitors to the Web site he uses to market it; he has only chilling reservations about the murders. "One good White man for just two dead muds is not a good trade," says Hale. "That's why it was a tragedy."

Giving Hate a Worldwide Audience

Some say that raising the profile of hate groups is perhaps not such a bad thing. Bringing them above ground where they can be seen, monitored, and to some extent countered, has its advantages. If that's the case, the Internet is doing the job.

No longer is organized racism the crude domain of shadowy Klansmen, street-corner skinheads, and furtive neo-Nazis meeting in basements and handing out cheap leaflets. White sheets and burning crosses have given way to Web servers and URLs, to Aryan chat rooms, and electronic archives of paranoid propaganda. Most of the 2,800 sites devoted to hate represent "groups" that are entirely Web-based: they would not exist if it weren't for the Internet. In this new age of intolerance, the Webmaster is the real grand dragon.

"The Internet is a major breakthrough for us. It's a significant advance to developing a White-rights movement in this country" Stormfront's creator, Don Black, has said. A one-time high-ranking Klansman who operates Stormfront from his home in West Palm Beach, Fla., Black has been using computer technology for nearly two decades. Having learned how to operate a Radio Shack TRS-80 in the early 1980s while serving a federal prison term for plotting to take over a Caribbean island for use as a homeland for White supremacists, Black now is considered the godfather of on-line hate. Stormfront has purportedly had more than 2.5 million hits since its inception. "It's almost like having a TV network," Black wrote on his home page in 1998.

But in bringing the hate industry to anyone's computer screen, making it as clickable as a recipe search on AltaVista or a Harry Potter order on Amazon.com, the information and technology revolution is unintentionally facilitating the spread of a cultural poison. In the United States, it comes in the form of protected free speech that is as likely to be slickly packaged and carefully cloaked in such euphemisms as "White heritage" or "White rights" as it is to feature cartoons of lynchings and blood-dripping images of caricatured Jews.

The men behind these Web sites are increasingly educated, articulate, and shrewd. Most are careful to avoid specific calls to violence and downplay their own menace, even as they rhapsodize about imploding the country's cultural and political structure with a bloody Racial Holy War—known in this subculture as "RaHoWa"—that they believe is necessary to achieve their dream of an Aryan America. The more militant among them have coined terms such as "leaderless resistance" and capitalized on the convergence of technology and the Constitution to adapt anarchy, once a largely leftist notion," to the extreme right-wing, racist agenda. Instructions for bomb making, for instance, are easily available on the Net.

With its infinite ability to create virtual communities, the Internet has also provided an unprecedented psychological link for once-isolated White supremacists. In the . . . summer [of 2000], after Senator Joseph Lieberman became the first Jewish person nominated for national office, chat rooms and message boards on America Online, Yahoo!, and CNN.com were peppered with anti-Semitic slurs. Officials scrambled to expunge the messages and ban the writers. Nowadays, even gay racists have a place to meet in cyberspace: "I'm glad this group is here" one member wrote in a recent posting on White Pride Gay Men, one of several Yahoo! clubs for irony-challenged homosexuals. "I'm sick and tired of niggers and Jews and tired of people thinking I'm 'tolerant' just 'cause I'm gay.'"

Targeting Generation "I"

"The Internet didn't create any of this stuff, but it gives people a sense empowerment," says Rabbi Abraham Cooper, associate dean of the Wiesenthal Center and a leader in the global fight against online hate. Cooper says the denizens of racist chat rooms and Web sites can come from any walk of life and any level of education. The anonymity of the Net makes it safe. He notes that he was recently invited to speak at the National Security Agency after officials discovered that staff members were exchanging racist e-mails. "Hate has been repackaged, and for the first time ever it's in the mainstream," Rabbi Cooper says. "The World Wide Web is the glue."

Of the greatest concern to those battling online hate is the ability of the Web sites to ensnare their primary target: young people, members of the first generation of the Information Age. "There's a lot of turnover in this movement," says Rick Eaton, Rabbi Cooper's chief researcher. "People come into it and get really consumed by it. They're told, 'We're gonna win, we're gonna accomplish our goals,' then they get frustrated and move on. So they constantly need new blood."

Handelsman. © 1998 by Tribune Media Services, Inc. Reprinted with permission.

Perhaps with that in mind, the National Alliance, branded "the single most dangerous organized hate group in the United States" by the Anti-Defamation League, purchased [in 2000] Resistance Records, an online marketer of hate music. The National Alliance is led by William Pierce, a physicist who is the author of the notorious right-wing extremist bible, *The Turner Diaries*, considered the inspiration for Oklahoma City bomber Timothy McVeigh.[2] The record company not only makes it easier for Pierce to reach young people, it helps finance his operations, which include a Web site and a weekly radio broadcast. Resistance Records sold 50,000 hate CDs in 1997, according to Rabbi Cooper, with titles such as "Too White for You" by the Angry Aryans.

Aiming at younger children, Matt Hale's World Church of the Creator features a children's page with crossword puzzles and games highlighting words that teach "racial loyalty." Words such as "nigger" and "kike." And Stormfront's kids' link, with music, games, a "history of the White race," and a poem ridiculing Blacks called "De Nite Fo' Crimmus" is the domain of founder Don Black's 12-year-old son, Derek. "White people are taught in school to be ashamed of their heritage," writes the boy, who is home-schooled. "Therefore, I think that now is the time that all of the White people across the globe should rise above the lies and be proud of who we are. To take back our freedom and win for all to see our heritage in its greatest glory."

"The youth are certainly the vanguard of the White racial loyalist movement," Matt Hale says from his home in East Peoria, Ill. "Half our members are 30 or younger and a quarter are under 20. We have people writing me saying, 'I'm 13 years old, can I join the church?' and, of course, I answer yes. People can join no matter how old they are. It means they have joined a community who have love for their own kind and hatred of their enemies and there's nothing more natural or beautiful than that."

Hate Site Staples

For the benefit of the young and old, most sites contain both state-of-the-art racism and traditional anti-Semitism. What seeps from the computer screen is a deep fear, even paranoia, about the rising prominence of African-Americans and immigrant minorities from Latin and Asian countries—the "mud races" as they are called—and about the prominence of Jews in media, commerce, and government. Overarching

2. William Pierce died on July 23, 2002.

it all is a loathing of what White Aryan Resistance leader Tom Metzger calls the "Iron Heel"—an American government that, in their view, is allowing, even promoting, the destruction of the White race.

Many sites contain endlessly repeated myths about Jews: that Benjamin Franklin declared at the Constitutional Convention that Jews were parasites and should be banned from the new country; that consumers pay a hidden "kosher tax" on food items; that the Federal Reserve is a Jewish conspiracy. Lists of American Jews in high places can be found on any number of sites, while Holocaust denial (and its variant, that the Holocaust didn't happen but that it should have) are also staples of hate sites.

And then there is Martinlutherking.org. It's a legitimate-looking site that appears on search engines such as Google.com and purports to be a primer on the life of Martin Luther King, Jr., with familiar photographs and reverent titles such as "The Death of the Dream." In fact, the site is a cleverly disguised collection of attacks on King's integrity, including some selective material from legitimate sources such as *Newsweek*. The site is the crafty work of Vincent Breeding, the 32-year-old Webmaster of several racist sites, including David Duke Online, the web site of the onetime grand wizard of the Ku Klux Klan. "How many kids find this site when they do their Martin Luther King essays in January?" asks Rabbi Cooper. "It's like the Flat Earth Society and CarlSagan.com—kids don't know the difference. There is no online librarian."

The Digital Battle

But there is an attempt to counter the propaganda with truth. Type "Benjamin Franklin" into a search engine, for instance, and you'll find a link to the ADL's Web site, where each of the anti-Semitic myths is exposed and refuted. The source of Franklin's purported statement, it reports, is a supposed diary by a member of the Constitutional Convention that has never been proven to exist. The ADL Web site is just one among several that are doing hard battle with the hate sites. All the major anti-bigotry organizations—the Wiesenthal Center and the Southern Poverty Law Center, along with the ADL—are now spending considerable resources fighting online hate, assigning staff members to constantly monitor activity and circulating their latest research on their sites, on CD-ROMs, and in print.

Other, lesser-known groups have emerged in cyberspace specifically to counter the Web-based hate groups. Hatewatch.org, which started out as a Harvard Law School library Web page, has become a forceful online civil rights group, offering up-to-date information about hate groups that use the Internet to recruit and organize, and taking active positions on situations involving bigotry.

They are all part of a digital guerilla war—a worldwide clash of philosophy and practicality involving the major Internet companies, public interest groups, people in law enforcement, and the courts. The battle rages from California, where federal prosecutors have won two convictions against men who sent threatening e-mails to Asian-Americans and Latinos—the first people prosecuted under the federal hate crime statute involving threats transmitted over the Internet—to France, where Yahoo! was recently found by a judge to have offended "the collective memory" of the country by allowing Nazi merchandise to appear on its auction site. Yahoo! subsequently decided to stop offering the merchandise, but is challenging the judge's order in American courts because of its broad implications. (The auction site eBay continues to offer racist material, but only if it is at least 50 years old, to allow for the collection of historical material. On a recent day, there were 2,775 Nazi items on the site and 136 featuring the Ku Klux Klan.) . . .

Filtering Out Racism

The notion that the major Internet providers are serving as portals to hate has pitted one kind of advocacy group against others. While the anti-bigotry groups want to at least marginalize the hate sites, others, like the American Civil Liberties Union and the Electronic Frontier Foundation, want to keep the Internet as free and open as possible. Some European countries outlaw certain bigoted material, but the Internet, of course, is borderless. That has led to this irony: The greatest source of Nazi material in Germany today is the United States.

The ADL, for one, recognizes the immutability of the Constitutional question, and offers another way to shield young people from hateful material. It sells a HateFilter software program that uses the technology of Cyber Patrol to block access to Web sites that advocate racial or ethnic hatred. Of course, it might well be that children whose parents care enough to buy a hate filter would be less susceptible to the influence of hate group in the first place. The real targets are those tech-savvy post-adolescents and young adults who could become the next Ben Smiths or Matthew Williams—the next lone wolves.

*"Neo-Nazis and skinheads, supported . . .
[by those with ties to] the right, continue
to recruit youngsters who lack parental
guidance and societal support."*

Alienation and Changing Sociopolitical Conditions Foster Hatred in Germany

Stephan Lhotzky

In the following viewpoint Stephan Lhotzky examines the reasons why hate groups have grown in Germany. Germany's hate groups have historical roots in Adolf Hitler's Nazi party, the author points out. After the demise of the Nazi party with the end of World War II, the problem of anti-Semitism was never openly challenged in East Germany. Furthermore, family bonds were weakened when East Germany's socialist government encouraged parents to send children to state-run day care centers. With the fall of communism and German reunification, many children have grown disaffected because they live in dysfunctional environments with little parental guidance. For some of these youths, the author explains, hate groups provide a sense of belonging. Lhotzky is a professor of German at Augustana College in Sioux Falls, South Dakota.

As you read, consider the following questions:

1. In what ways was life easier for the average citizen in socialist East Germany as compared to today's Germany, according to the author?
2. In Lhotzky's opinion, why is the United States a bad model for Europe to follow in addressing hate crimes?

Stephan Lhotzky, "Will Kai Become a Skinhead?" *Reclaiming Children and Youth*, vol. 10, Summer 2001, p. 86. Copyright © 2001 by *Reclaiming Children and Youth*. Reproduced by permission.

W hen I first met Kai,[1] he was 11 years old and living with his mother in a small fourth-floor apartment in the former socialist housing development called Schlaatz in Potsdam, Germany. Kai's mother was employed at a local supermarket, but her husband had left the family a few years earlier. Kai began to develop discipline problems in school, which seemed to start about the time his father disappeared. Because Kai was not completing homework assignments and was coming to class unprepared, Kai's mother was asked to attend a number of parent-teacher conferences, which were held in the presence of all the parents of the children in Kai's class. At each meeting, problem cases among the students were discussed openly, a practice common in the former German Democratic Republic. Repeatedly, Kai's mother was asked about her son's problems. At each meeting, she became more frustrated with the teacher's comments: "Ms. P., your son is not making the necessary progress at this level. Frankly, I don't know anymore what to do with him. He is inattentive in class and disrupts my teaching."

Although this format of open discussion was familiar to Kai's mother, she became increasingly defensive and pointed out that she was a single mother, had a full-time job, and had little time to ensure that Kai was completing his homework on time. The group discussions led nowhere. Kai's case would be brought up each time, and then the teacher would move on to other topics.

Kai's mother was able to describe her own difficulties, but her son had little say in the process, other than to reply to his mother's questions during dinner that he would improve his performance. Ms. P. eventually stopped attending the frustrating and useless conferences and began to ignore notes from the school that increasingly detailed Kai's disruptive and antisocial behavior in and out of class. In fact, it had progressed to a point where Kai was physically attacking younger students.

During this time, I and my family were living in the same complex (I was on sabbatical from Augustana College), so we

---

1. During his year at the Schlaatz, the author had the opportunity to observe many young people from this housing development. Kai is a composite of these youths.

were able to observe much of Kai's behavior. Kai began to lead a double life. In the evening, he managed to maintain the role of a well-behaved child who loves his mother. But while he succeeded in making his mother believe that he was simply struggling with the school's academic curriculum, he was involved in behavior that increasingly escalated from simple pranks to more delinquent outbursts. At first, he would go down into the basement of the housing complex and let the air out of residents' bicycle tires. Then he began using a knife to slash the tires. He scattered trash from the garbage containers on the street while building residents watched, fearful of reacting to his belligerent attitude. Kai started to harass younger elementary school children on their way to school, even when a parent accompanied them. He would throw apples and rocks at the adults from a distance, and one time threw bottles at toddlers from his apartment window while his mother was at work.

Whenever angry neighbors confronted Kai's mother, she would call Kai to come to the door, but each time he eloquently denied any wrongdoing. Kai's actions thus engendered no consequences. The adult world of postreunification eastern Germany was silent, unable to deal with him and many other children in the desolate and dysfunctional environment of the ghastly housing developments that are a remnant of East Germany socialism.

Kai's problems are representative of the difficulties faced by many children and adolescents in eastern Germany during the past 10 years following German reunification. Kai's behavior is a textbook example of a child's reaction to threatening changes in his personal environment. The incomprehensible breakdown of his family situation fostered defiance and destructiveness. Neither Kai's mother nor the school authorities were able or willing to act when the first warning signs began to appear. Four years ago, Kai was a "problem child" out on the streets and parking lots between the buildings of the housing developments—places where young skinheads and neo-Nazis would congregate, deciding whether they should just hang out or do some damage. Police patrols in these areas were rare.

Kai was a troubled child in an environment capable of

drawing him into the arms of a hate group. Today, Kai is 15 years old. Although it is unknown whether he has joined any right-wing radical group, it would not be surprising if he has. Today, neo-Nazis in Potsdam have declared the Schlaatz housing development to be "nationally liberated," meaning that no foreigners live in it. Reliable statistics about the activities of neo-Nazis and other extremist right-wing groups in Germany are rare and often contradictory, so trying to obtain information about Kai's status is difficult.

Falling into the Trap of Hatred

The fascination with strange and seemingly mythical rituals as well as the "adventure" that illegal activities promised caused Carla and her adolescent daughter, Tina, to become part of the neo-Nazi scene in Germany. Carla had just gone through a difficult divorce, and her husband had played a minor role in the NPD (the right-wing National Party of Germany). Carla thus was familiar with antiforeigner attitudes and the denial of the Holocaust.

Carla and her daughter were invited by Nazi contacts to attend a solstice celebration put on by right-wing extremists. In the middle of a forest near Pirmasens, a bonfire was built, and an organizer instructed Carla to wear a white sheet, purportedly "consecrated 3 weeks earlier," so that she would be "properly" clad when she recited the ritualistic "fire words" later in the ceremony. Groups of skinheads sat around the bonfire drinking homemade "mead." When they eventually stood together in smaller circles to masturbate, Carla was disappointed by her decision to be present at this event.

Hans, a neo-Nazi who resembled Adolph Hitler down to his moustache and hairstyle, was able to restore Carla's faith in neo-Nazism by speaking to her about the "movement" in a most convincing and enthusiastic way. Hans was not a skinhead—he was a fanatic whose childhood had been dominated by anti-Semitic slogans uttered by his strict Catholic father. Like Carla at the Pirmasens' bonfire, Hans had always felt uneasy when dealing with skinheads, who to him were simply an unkempt group of people; however, he realized their importance in the "national fight" and therefore put up with their undisciplined behavior. When he became a soldier in the German army, Hans propagated action against "Jewish pigs" and was immediately dismissed.

On the night of the Pirmasens bonfire, Hans fell in love with Carla. Hans, Carla, and Tina began defiling and damaging Jewish cemeteries. Eventually Carla began to question their actions, but by that time it was too late. All three were arrested and faced prison terms of up to 5 years.

The Part Politics Plays

The general milieu of neo-Nazis in Germany and other countries is one that appeals to people who are frustrated by a pluralism that seems to have left them out of the loop. Many times, those frustrations are deeply rooted in personal experiences of failure that are then projected onto a seemingly disorderly, permissive society. Neo-Nazism also draws in individuals who are fascinated by virtually any aspect of historical National Socialism in Germany, among them the philosophy of political and social "order," the concept of racial purity, the Fuehrer principle, and the fascination with "mythical" rituals—all taken from Third Reich propaganda. . . .

Although they often collaborate with and frequently are recruited by neo-Nazis, skinheads know very little about the neo-Nazi organization. Most skinheads have the bare minimum required education and are employed in low-wage jobs. Because unemployment is high, they feel helpless and hopeless regarding their future, and they resort to physical violence in reaction. The ever-present alcohol abuse among skinheads dramatically increases their willingness to employ brutal, violent behavior. Unlike neo-Nazis, skinheads in Germany and other countries find it difficult to formulate a common program; if they feel unity, it is in their common frustration, and they rarely articulate goals in a consistent way. The Web site homepage of the Italian "Skinhead Girls," which is a hodgepodge of information, is typical of skinheads throughout Europe. It is a collective of very different political positions: "We are against corrupted society, drug culture, genetic manipulations, abortion, and scumbags!" The final motto has almost altruistic overtones: "Work all together for growing better."

Fueling the aggressions of both neo-Nazis and skinheads

are individual representatives of political parties, such as some candidates for public office of the CDU (Christian Democratic Party, the party of former Chancellor Helmut Kohl) as well as entire political party programs of the Republikaner (Republicans) or of the NPD (the National Party of Germany). Jorg Haider's Austrian Freedom Party is also known for its carefully worded anti-immigrant positions. Some political figures in other European countries contribute to the understandable, yet completely irrational, xenophobia. During the first half of the 1990s, Germany had the highest immigration numbers in Europe; however, although antiforeigner violence continues to increase, immigration numbers have been dropping since 1995. A hate group from the Schlaatz housing development in Potsdam does not exist in a vacuum or without reason. Neo-Nazis and skinheads, supported in spirit—and probably with financial backing—by individuals with some ties to political parties of the right, continue to recruit youngsters who lack parental guidance and societal support.

Why Hate Groups Have Grown

Right-wing extremist groups, whether they subscribe to the rigidly structured neo-Nazi orchestrations of violence or the spiteful reactions of skinheads, have nothing to offer an educated adult person. But to young people like Kai, such a group insinuates that it offers what his mother may be unable to give him: the care and nurturing of a functioning family. ... For Kai and other youngsters in unstable social situations, such groups provide. . . a strong sense of belonging. . . .

Understanding the social mechanisms at work in cases such as Kai's is but one part of the whole. What other arenas must be addressed?

Historical. The current right-wing extremist movement in Europe has historical roots in German National Socialism and Hitler's Third Reich. After the end of World War II and the demise of Nazi Germany, National Socialism survived in both East Germany and West Germany during the "Cold War" era. In communist East Germany, for example, the end of the Third Reich was touted as a victory of one political system (Communism) over the other (National Socialism).

An open discussion about anti-Semitism, an important ingredient of Nazi propaganda, never took place in East Germany. In West Germany, a former member of the Nazi Party was able to rise to the position of federal chancellor, the West German head of state. Although West Germany instigated a thorough and ongoing public discussion of Hitler's Third Reich, the conversation took place only at certain levels. Countries such as Sweden and Switzerland have been made aware of their involvement with Nazi Germany only recently.

Female Skinheads

Although the vast majority of [German] far-right activists are male, experts believe that the growing influx of women is dangerous. Robert Bihler, from Bavaria's Office for the Protection of the Constitution, fears that the strong membership fluctuation among the hitherto predominantly male skinhead groups will decrease now that the young men no longer have to look for partners outside the group. Instead of leaving the gang after a couple of years to settle down, they will stay in the group. Thus, "the scene will solidify," says Bihler. Moreover, since women don't fit the popular neo-Nazi stereotype, "the more [who] enter the scene, the less negative its image will become," warns, [sociologist Renate] Bitzan. Girl power, it seems, isn't necessarily a good thing.

Time International, May 7, 2001.

Sociohistorical. The sociohistorical factor played an important role in the development of right-wing extremism in postreunification Germany, including the difficulty in switching from one political system to another virtually overnight. Life in socialist East Germany was indeed easier for the average citizen than it is today in a united Germany. The state, the government, the party, and the system provided for every person. Jobs were secure; officially, there was hardly any crime and life was safe. The social net, with its free medical care and many other benefits such as schooling, after-school care, and daycare for infants, was provided by the government. In East Germany many of the difficult decisions families in a democracy must make were unnecessary.

By providing for the family, East German government

agencies also assumed a parenting role, a process that was in the best interest of the state. The government understood that in order to ensure support of socialism by the next generation, socialist ideology had to be inculcated early—in young children. Both parents were encouraged to work. Infants were watched, toddlers potty-trained, and school-age children supervised while they completed homework assignments in state-run daycare institutions. Because the parents were at work, somebody else took care of the children—a situation very similar to that in the United States today. East Germany also experienced a high divorce rate. The traditional family with its real and imaginary values was disappearing. Whenever there is a decrease in parenting responsibilities and this process translates into heightened convenience for the parents, the bond between parents and children will be weakened. As a result, children and adolescents in East Germany are particularly susceptible to efforts by groups that purport to act as parental substitutes.

Economics. [M.] Yamba pointed out that unemployment is the only consistent factor that visibly correlates with anti-foreigner attitudes in Europe today. At this point, there is little statistical evidence of other correlations in regard to aggression directed against foreigners, in part due to a lack of time necessary to developing extensive studies. There has been decade-long neglect in examining the threat hate groups pose to European societies.

Possible Remedies

In light of the current situation, with a dramatic rise in hate crimes committed by right-wing extremists, remedies that are developed must address all of the previously mentioned factors. Attempts to resolve only one portion of the problem are destined to fail. The current political leadership in Germany has finally recognized the problem as serious and threatening to the very foundation of state and society, but legally banning the right-wing NPD party will not correct the situation and may have an adverse effect by making martyrs out of neo-Nazis. A sudden and massive educational effort in regard to National Socialist thinking may be needed, but positive results from such an effort will take more than a few years to occur. Experienced social workers trained in conflict-management strategies must engage young people in areas such as the Schlaatz housing development in Potsdam, but the work cannot be left to them alone. Economists must develop strategies to reduce unemployment in the long term and not encourage politicians to manipulate unemployment statistics, a common practice in Germany.

Experts in a variety of fields will need to work together, and individuals and groups must contribute in ways that transcend narrow lines of perceived responsibilities. Educators and social workers must learn to cooperate with political scientists, and historians will need to acquire the skills to collaborate with economists and child development professionals. The 20th-century focus on specialization without broader perspectives must be abandoned. No longer can specialists remain specialists without understanding other areas and disciplines. If Europe is to master the current crisis, it must remember its rich educational tradition, in particular the concept of humanism, which includes a model of education that propagates specialization and the ability to synthesize areas of specialty at the same time. The product of that type of education will be a well-rounded individual educated in the liberal arts.

Europe Is on Its Own

The European Union has yet to find a way of proactively and effectively dealing with the problem of right-wing extremism, and although the United States has been projecting the image of a leader in world affairs, it is unable to provide orientation at this juncture in European development. A nation that quite visibly and unmistakably permits children to be bombarded by media images of violence, that arbitrarily changes its own rules, tries juvenile offenders as adults, and perceives rigorous punishment to be the only solution to crime can hardly serve as a model for Europe in regard to hate crimes. Europe is on its own. Europe must find solutions quickly. Unfortunately for Kai and others like him, it may be too late.

Periodical Bibliography

The following articles have been selected to supplement the diverse views presented in this chapter.

Les Back	"White Fortresses in Cyberspace," *UNESCO Courier*, January 2001.
Stacia Brown	"Virtual Hate," *Sojourners*, September/October 2000.
David Cullen	"Bullies in the Pulpit," *In These Times*, November 29, 1998.
Ivo H. Daalder and Paul Gottfried	"Should Americans Be Concerned About the Rise of Far-Right Parties in Europe?" (Symposium), *Insight*, June 3, 2002.
Mike Davis	"The Devil's Ranchos," *ColorLines*, Winter 2001/2002.
Mark Flanigan	"Coming Out of Hatred," *Advocate*, July 4, 2000.
Guerry Hoddersen	"The High Price of Ignoring Teen-Age Fascists," *People's Weekly World*, May 29, 1999.
Doug Johnson	"Former Recruiter for Racism Helps Military Confront Hate," *Washington Post*, August 28, 2000.
David Kirby	"What's in a Basher's Mind?" *Advocate*, September 28, 1999.
Martin E. Marty, interviewed by Camille Colatosti	"Is It Possible to Get Along with Fundamentalists?" *Witness*, December 2001.
James P. Pinkerton	"Evil's Allure Gives Life to Nazi Chic," *Los Angeles Times*, April 20, 2001.
Ralph Raico	"Nazifying the Germans," *Rothbard-Rockwell Report*, October 1999.
Gary S. Rotto and Kenneth S. Stern	"The Link Between America's Hatemongers," *San Diego Union-Tribune*, August 13, 1999.
Rosemary Radford Ruether	"Racist Extremists Use Bible Verses to Justify Killing," *National Catholic Reporter*, August 27, 1999.
Thandeka	"The Cost of Whiteness," *Tikkun*, May/June 1999.

CHAPTER 3

Do Certain Groups Pose a Threat to Tolerance?

Chapter Preface

During the late twentieth century the United States witnessed an apparent increase in the number of groups advocating white supremacy, anti-Semitism, and racial separatism. These groups include revived chapters of the Ku Klux Klan, various neo-Nazi factions, and loosely organized gangs of racist skinheads. Many believe that the proliferation of such groups is facilitated by the ease and low cost of Internet communications, and that a growing white supremacist influence will lead to an increase in hate crimes and domestic terrorism in the twenty-first century. According to Methodist pastor and teacher Peter DeGroote, "The [white supremacist] movement has interpreted changing economic and political conditions through a reformulation of old fears, hatreds, and conspiracy theories. Like a virus once thought under control, ideas and hatreds that racked the 20th century have mutated, ready to infect a new century."

One disturbing white supremacist notion is the concept of "RAHOWA," or racial holy war, an apocalyptic conflict between "Aryans" and nonwhites that many neo-Nazis believe will usher in a "new world order" and a future white kingdom. As DeGroote explains, neo-Nazis see diversity, pluralism, and civil rights as a threat to white dominion, and have concluded "that it is necessary to overthrow the United States government before any further damage can be done." In addition, notes DeGroote, many neo-Nazis are convinced that such a coup "can be accomplished in this century, some believing it possible within 25 years."

Other experts, however, contend that these neo-Nazi threats are largely harmless. In the opinion of David A. Lehrer, director of a California chapter of the Anti-Defamation League, racist and anti-Semitic hate groups do not pose a significant threat in a society that values tolerance and diversity. He maintains that "the nether world of hate has a very limited and narrowly defined constituency that, in large part, acts out of a . . . desperate attempt to attract media and public attention." Although several hate-group members have committed violent crimes, Lehrer believes that these crimes are isolated incidents that do not reflect popular opinion or have the support of any organized political movement. The white supremacist world is "a minutely small, incestuous circle of ideological soul mates who . . . speak mainly to themselves," says Lehrer. "They have no potential of being a serious political force or of galvanizing American public opinion." Instead of overreacting to white supremacist threats, Lehrer and other experts suggest that Americans continue to educate their children about tolerance "so that the potential audience for bigots . . . is ever smaller."

Social analysts and other concerned observers have differing opinions on the nature and extent of the danger posed by white supremacist groups and other extremist or radical organizations. The authors in the following chapter offer further discussion on whether such groups are a threat to a tolerant society.

1

*"The [hate-group] war may soon become
more organized—and worse."*

Hate Groups Are a Serious Threat

Carl Rowan

Shootings and bombings committed by white supremacists
reveal how dangerous hate groups can be, writes syndicated
columnist Carl Rowan in the following viewpoint. Although
these crimes have thus far been isolated incidents, they have
been praised by well-known hate-group leaders and may be
harbingers of a more organized "race war" in the years to
come, argues Rowan. Americans must come to understand
that hate groups pose a serious threat, he concludes.

As you read, consider the following questions:

1. According to Rowan, what did the leader of the Aryan
   Nations say about Buford O. Furrow after his summer
   1999 shooting rampage?
2. What was the topic of Rowan's 1996 book?
3. What tactics are hate groups now using to reach high
   schools, colleges, and the military, according to the
   author?

Carl Rowan, "The Creeping Race War," *Liberal Opinion Week*, vol. 10, August 30,
1999, p. 10. Copyright © 1999 by North American Syndicate. Reproduced by
permission.

[In 1999] after Buford O. Furrow shot five people at a Jewish community center in Los Angeles and gunned down postal worker Joseph Ileto because "he was nonwhite and worked for the federal government," the white supremacist leader of the Idaho-based Aryan Nations said of Furrow: "He was a good soldier."

"I cannot condemn what he did. He was very respected among us," added Richard Butler, leader of a group that is notorious for advocating violence as a means of making the United States an all-white nation.

Not Just Lone Wolves

Butler's words suggest that Furrow was not just a deranged loner when he launched his attack on Jews and nonwhites. Just as Benjamin Nathaniel Smith was more than a loner when he staged a shooting attack on Jews, blacks and Asians in Illinois and Indiana over the [1999] Fourth of July weekend. Just as Timothy J. McVeigh and Terry L. Nichols were not just "lone wolf" nuts when they perpetrated the 1995 bombing of the Alfred P. Murrah federal building in Oklahoma City, killing 168 people.

The bigots within America who hate blacks, Jews, "foreigners," immigrants, Muslims and the federal government are carrying out an unholy war, but it is a war of snipers, isolated shootings and bombings, and one-man forays so far. It may soon become more organized—and worse.

So it is wise that Columbine High School in Colorado reopens this week [in August 1999] under conditions of heightened security. It is prudent that schools across America have taken steps to prevent outbursts of violence by those caught in the dark clutches of the haters. It would be well for the rest of us to be on guard.

The Coming Race War

In 1996, I published a book warning that this society was imperiled by white racists who threatened to kill Jews, deport or kill blacks, wage war on unfavorable judges and federal facilities, and eventually provoke a tragic race war. I made the mistake of titling that book *The Coming Race War in America*, thus scaring the hell out of many reviewers and people who branded it "alarmist" without reading it. I cited the 800 or so "militias" and the assorted venomous groups in America that had made as their "bible" a book by William Pierce called *The Turner Diaries*, in which the script for the Oklahoma City bombing was set forth in chilling detail. That book also set forth a plan for the extermination of blacks, Jews and unwanted immigrants.

My "alarmist" book is more pertinent, its documentation more chilling, today than it was in 1996, because the haters have their war more on track. I am more alarmed now that I have seen Tom Metzger, leader of California's White Aryan Resistance (WAR), declare, "Good hunting, lone wolves" as he calls for a second civil war in exhorting his soldiers to act "in any way you see fit" against immigrants. The "crazy" single killers all have commanders giving orders.

EVERY ONCE IN AWHILE IT BACKS UP

Stantis. © 1999 by *The Birmingham News*. Reprinted by permission of Copley News Service.

Since 1995, the FBI and other law enforcement agencies have moved against the Viper Militia and other paramilitary groups that were amassing illegal arms and clearly constituted a threat of violence. That provoked a movement away from group actions. To foil FBI and police infiltrators, as I predicted in my book, the move has been to "lone wolf" and "good soldier" violence, with Internet and telephone messages and books by Pierce and other racists setting forth the battle cries and the targets.

The "race war" advocates are now reaching high schools, colleges and official military units through the Internet in ways they never could through books and pamphlets. Thus they have exposed us all to the threat of sudden death.

The problem America faces is far beyond the need to get psychiatrists to a small number of "sick" souls. It is not enough for schools, synagogues, black churches and non-white facilities to increase security. We must somehow get all of white America out of denial about the magnitude of "Christian Identity" racism and madness in this society.

The "disciples" and "soldiers" of Butler and Metzger will kill anyone—anyone—they think stands in the way of their Aryan America. Their race war is on. We can waste no time learning more about who they are and where they next plan to strike. And our law enforcement people must act accordingly.

> "*I worry about laying blame at [the]
> doorstep [of hate groups]. Such
> organizations can be more easily
> stigmatized than understood.*"

Stigmatizing Hate Groups as a Threat May Be Counterproductive

Anthony B. Robinson

In the following viewpoint Anthony B. Robinson warns that the crimes of isolated individuals who are connected with hate groups may lead to a stigmatization of and overreaction against such groups. Moreover, Robinson maintains, society may be overlooking the role that mental illness can play in hate crimes. For example, Buford Furrow Jr., who opened fire on a Jewish community center in 1999, was suffering from an untreated mental illness. But rather than facing the challenge of mental illness, many experts prefer to lay the blame for such crimes on white supremacist groups. Demonizing these groups can in turn lead to regrettable actions against them, the author points out. Robinson is pastor of the Plymouth Congregational Church in Seattle, Washington.

As you read, consider the following questions:
1. According to the author, what "warning signals" pointed to Larry Gene Ashbrooks's mental illness?
2. The mentally ill make up what percentage of the homeless population, according to Robinson?
3. What three basic lessons has Robinson learned about mental illness and its treatment?

Anthony B. Robinson, "Violence and Illness," *Christian Century*, vol. 116, October 20, 1999, p. 990. Copyright © 1999 by the Christian Century Foundation. Reproduced by permission.

When violence breaks out and murder occurs, we want an explanation, a reason, and preferably someone to blame. After Buford Furrow shot children at a Jewish day-care center and then a Filipino-American postal worker in Los Angeles [in August 1999], the media trained its sights on the Idaho-based Aryan Nations, to which Furrow belonged. Full-page stories with color pictures took us into the lair and the mind of Aryan Nations founder Richard Butler. [Later that year], after Larry Gene Ashbrook opened fire at Wedgewood Baptist Church in Fort Worth, reports surfaced about his link with an Aryan Nations-like group known as the Phineas Priesthood.

I think we need to monitor such groups. I am glad that the Southern Poverty Law Center and similar watchdog agencies report on the activities of organized hate groups. Yet I worry about laying blame at their doorstep. Such organizations can be more easily stigmatized than understood. And it is not difficult to come to the conclusion that such groups are a social malignancy, candidates for surgical removal. The catastrophe at Waco with the Branch Davidians[1] ought to caution us against simply stigmatizing offensive groups. Sometimes we can get so scared of something that we end up doing things we ought not to do, things that we regret.

The Role of Mental Illness

Explaining the Buford Furrows and Larry Gene Ashbrooks of the world by pointing to hate groups can also obscure the role that mental illness plays in these terrible incidents. Before Furrow made his fateful trip to Los Angeles his family had sought help, even hospitalization, for him. They did not get it. For anyone with even a rudimentary knowledge of mental illness and its symptoms, Ashbrook's story was full of warning signals. Neighbors described a man given to sudden mood swings and outbursts of anger, a man who had just sustained the loss of his father. Ashbrook's letters to newspapers and radio stations in Fort Worth were replete with paranoid

---

1. In April 1993, after a long standoff, federal agents raided the complex of the extremist Branch Davidian cult near Waco, Texas. More than eighty people died during this operation.

fantasies and accounts of hearing voices. Yet the media reports did not emphasize mental illness. Instead we heard about the Phineas priests. We heard professors from Southwestern Baptist Theological Seminary speaking of the battle with Satan. And we heard [then] Governor George W. Bush say that what we're up against here is "evil."

We are by and large terribly ignorant about mental illness. It scares us. We have done a poor job not only in educating people about mental illness but in treating those who suffer from it and in supporting their families.

This is not to suggest that those who suffer mental illness are inherently more prone to violence than others, or that the solution is to criminalize and imprison them. There is already entirely too much recourse to that, often by default, since people with a mental illness often go untreated. Eventually some of them commit a crime and end up in jail where they remain untreated. A significant percentage of our swollen prison population is made up of people with untreated mental illness.

The Need for Social Support

Mental illness and those who suffer from it are often shrouded in ignorance, fear, shame and isolation. Those suffering from schizophrenia, bipolar disorder or major depression are often not receiving either medical treatment or social support.

For several decades we have been fashioning a social ethic that says, "You're on your own." One is reminded of the passage in the Letter of James: "If a brother or sister is ill-clad and in lack of daily food, and one of you says to them, 'Go in peace, be warmed and filled,' without giving them the things needed for the body, what does it profit?"

In his 1995 study, *Surviving Schizophrenia—A Family Manual*, E. Fuller Torrey estimates that 90 percent of those who would have been in psychiatric hospitals 40 years ago, before deinstitutionalization really got under way, are not hospitalized today. A significant number live with their families, families which themselves are often isolated and drained by the task of caring for them. Many of those who suffer mental illnesses live alone. And many, far too many,

Mental Illness Writes the Script

It is possible that some people who are suffering from some forms of mental illness become caught up in political or religious subcultures where apocalyptic thinking and demonization are commonplace. They then lack the psychological restraints that keep other similarly situated people from acting out on their beliefs in a violent manner. . . .

For example, [consider] the case of John C. Salvi III, who shot abortion providers in Boston. Salvi came out of an apocalyptic Catholic Right subculture. Salvi was someone who was arguably mentally ill, but who picked his targets based on a recognizable political/theological outlook. The same may be true with Buford Furrow, Jr. who shot up a Jewish day care center in California, then killed a Filipino-American postal worker. Furrow came out of an apocalyptic neonazi subculture that demonized Jews, people of color, and the government. The political/theological outlook sets the stage, but it is the mental illness that writes the script where someone pulls the trigger or commits other acts of violence.

Chip Berlet, www.publicye.org, 2003.

live on the streets and in homeless shelters. By most estimates the mentally ill make up 40 to 50 percent of the homeless population. It does not, as they say, take a rocket scientist to see that a significant number of the people haunting street corners and alleys are our brothers and sisters who are ill. Imagine deciding that we would put 90 percent of all cancer patients out on the street!

A Few Basic Lessons

I speak not only as a minister who has worked with persons experiencing mental illness and with their families, but as one who has gone through a severe depression and who has mental illness in his family. Mental illness is a complex matter: I am not a mental health professional. But I have learned a few basic lessons about the illness and its treatment:

First, the brain is an organ of the body. Like the kidney or the heart, the brain can get sick. The brain may be traumatized by loss or violence. Or there can be too many or too few of certain chemicals necessary for proper functioning. The result is a disorder in thinking, mood and behavior.

Such disorders do not reflect a character defect or a moral

failure; they reflect an illness. Those suffering from a mental illness are not bad people. Indeed, part of the heartache for their families is that they are often quite extraordinary and gifted people.

Second, mental illnesses are treatable. Medication, in concert with social support, can help many people regain normal functioning, much the way insulin and diet can allow a diabetic to manage that illness.

Third, despite variations in law and treatment from state to state, people suffering from mental illness are usually able to refuse treatment until it can be shown that they constitute a threat to themselves or to others. If they climb to the top of bridge or have a knife in their hand, then something can be done, but not until then.

This means that much of the time treatment comes too late. And often treatment is of such short duration that the cycle of illness repeats itself. There has to be a humane middle ground between locking people up and the looking the other way or walking faster past them.

"*In the wake of 9/11 there are plenty of highly charged racial issues for the far right to inflame and exploit.*"

The Far Right Poses a Threat

Daniel Levitas

In the wake of the September 11, 2001, terrorist attacks, the far right has stepped up efforts to strengthen the resolve of its core supporters, maintains Daniel Levitas in the following viewpoint. Anti-Semitic hate groups hailed the September 11 terrorists for killing Jews in New York City, yet these groups still promote bigoted views of Arabs and Muslims, Jews' traditional enemies. Some among the Christian Right have used the tragedy as a pretext to denounce Muslims, Arab immigrants, liberals, and homosexuals, whom they claim have contributed to America's decline. In addition, former militia members are increasingly lending their support to political candidates who advocate white nationalism. Levitas is the author of *The Terrorist Next Door: The Militia Movement and the Radical Right* and has testified about racist, anti-Semitic and neo-Nazi groups as an expert witness in American and Canadian courts since 1986.

As you read, consider the following questions:

1. What did National Alliance organizer Billy Roper say about the September 11, 2001, terrorist attacks, according to the author?
2. According to Levitas, how did some Christian Right leaders interpret the events of September 11?
3. What candidate ran on a white Christian nationalist platform in the 2000 presidential race, according to Levitas?

Daniel Levitas, "The Radical Right After 9/11," *Nation*, vol. 275, July 22–29, 2002, pp. 19–23. Copyright © 2002 The Nation Magazine/The Nation Company, Inc. Reproduced by permission of the publisher and the author.

"Hallelu-Yahweh! May the WAR be started! DEATH to His ene-mies, may the World Trade Center BURN TO THE GROUND! . . . We can blame no others than ourselves for our problems due to the fact that we allow . . . Satan's children, called jews [sic] today, to have dominion over our lives. . . . My suggestion to all brethren, if we are left alone, sit back and watch the death throws [sic] of this Babylonian beast system and later we can get involved in clean up operations. If this beast system looks to us to plunder, arrest and fill their detention camps with, then by all means fight force with force and leave not a man standing!"

—"Pastor" August B. Kries III, Sheriff's Posse Comitatus

The attacks of September 11 [2001] focused the nation's attention on terrorist threats from abroad, but even as the World Trade Center towers were collapsing, hate groups were scheming about how to turn the situation to their advantage in the United States. "WONDERFUL NEWS, BROTH-ERS!!" crowed Hardy Lloyd, the Pittsburgh coordinator of the racist, anti-Semitic World Church of the Creator. Refer-encing ZOG—the supposed "Zionist Occupied Govern-ment" of the United States—Lloyd alerted supporters throughout western Pennsylvania on September 12 that "maybe as many as 10,000 Zoggites are dead." He also called for vigilante street violence. "The war is upon us all, time to get shooting lone wolves!! [September 11] is a wonderful day for us all. . . . Let's kick some Jew ass."

Lloyd and other militants may have been excited by the suicidal hijackers of Al Qaeda, but like the Oklahoma City bombing six years earlier, the events of 9/11 enraged the American public and undermined those on the radical right devoted to criminal violence. Additionally, fear and resent-ment over the prospect of heightened government surveil-lance has prompted numerous rightists to denounce the pas-sage of antiterrorism legislation, while others are mulling over whether to go underground. "The Feds are clamping down with the definition of a domestic terrorist," warned Christopher Kenney, the "Commander" of the Republic of Texas, a "Christian Patriot" group whose original leaders are serving long prison terms for earlier crimes. "I am sure there will be even more restrictions coming down the pike. We must prepare while we can."

Although most of the Christian right has avoided the kind

of violent antigovernment rhetoric embraced by many neo-Nazis after 9/11, some have not. Militant antiabortion campaigners were quick to take advantage of public fears by mailing hundreds of letters containing fake anthrax to family planning clinics across the nation. And homophobes like the Rev. Fred Phelps of Topeka, Kansas, celebrated 9/11 by gleefully declaring that "the Rod of God hath smitten fag America!" and "the multitudes slain Sept. 11, 2001 are in Hell—forever!" The response was different from Christian Coalition founder Pat Robertson and other more mainstream leaders of the religious right, but they also tried to turn the tragedy to their political advantage by attacking Arab immigrants, Islam, liberals, feminists, gays and other enemies both secular and allegedly profane. As for militia and "patriot" groups—whose numbers have been dwindling since the late 1990s—some seized on events to unload their inventory of survivalist paraphernalia left over from the marketing bust of Y2K, while others proclaimed their loyalty to the Republic—or threatened to overthrow it.

Bloodthirsty endorsements of 9/11 won't win hate groups many recruits. But like the conspiracy theories hatched after Oklahoma City (i.e., that Timothy McVeigh was a government patsy who killed 168 people to give the New World Order a pretext to repress the patriot movement), many of the statements made by right-wing militants have been aimed at hardening the movement faithful, not attracting those on the outside looking in. As others on the radical right have done, Hardy Lloyd both praised and vilified the September 11 hijackers. "My only concern is that we Aryans didn't do this and that the rag-heads are ahead of us on the Lone Wolf point scale." Other neo-Nazis called the attackers "towel heads" and worse yet, hailed them as "very brave people [who] were willing to die for whatever they believed in."

"We may not want them marrying our daughters. . . . But anyone who is willing to drive a plane into a building to kill Jews is alright by me. I wish our members had half as much testicular fortitude," observed Billy Roper, deputy membership coordinator of the National Alliance. Notwithstanding such anti-Arab bigotry, some leaders of the radical right believe that 9/11 is a good reason to make common cause with radical Islamic fundamentalists and others who share their visceral hatred of Jews and Israel, though it is unlikely a functional alliance will be formed.

Anti-Arab Sentiments

Militant anti-Semites like Roper may be willing to join forces with America's enemies in the hopes of overthrowing ZOG, but in the aftermath of the terrorist attacks the targets of vigilante violence were not Jews but Arabs and others mistaken for Middle Easterners. In the ten weeks following 9/11, the American-Arab Anti-Discrimination Committee reported more than 500 violent incidents, including threats, assaults, arsons, shootings and at least a half-dozen murders. Attacks on South Asian immigrants spiked sharply, with about 250 incidents reported in the last three months of 2001 alone.

Bigotry and intolerance have hardly been limited to criminals, mobs and hate groups. On February 21 [2001] Pat Robertson denounced Islam on the Christian Broadcasting Network's *700 Club*, saying it "is not a peaceful religion that wants to coexist. They want to coexist until they can control, dominate and then if need be destroy." Robertson asserted that US immigration policies are "so skewed to the Middle East and away from Europe that we have introduced these people into our midst and undoubtedly there are terrorist cells all over them."

Robertson's remarks came on the heels of criticism of US Attorney General John Ashcroft for statements he made [in] November [2001] disparaging Islam. In a radio interview with Cal Thomas, a conservative pundit and syndicated columnist, Ashcroft reportedly said that "Islam is a religion in which God requires you to send your son to die for him. Christianity is a faith in which God sends his son to die for you." Thomas published Ashcroft's statements on November 9, but it wasn't until Muslim groups discovered Thomas's column in early February [2002] that the resulting controversy reached the pages of the *Washington Post*. Ashcroft's response—that his reported statements "do not accurately reflect what I believe I said"—has done little to allay Arab-American concerns.

111

Similar anti-Arab sentiments have been voiced by the Council of Conservative Citizens [CCC], a white supremacist group descended from the Citizens' Council movement, which vigorously opposed integration in the 1950s and '60s. Praised by former member Trent Lott [a Republican senator from Mississippi], the CCC produces literature and a website overflowing with racist rhetoric venerating the Confederacy and railing against "black militants, alien parasites, queer activists . . . Christ haters" and multiculturalism. Predictably, the council has also taken to spewing anti-Arab and anti-immigrant bigotry, denouncing "Dirty Rotten Arabs and Muslims" and blaming 9/11 on pluralism and the nation's alleged "open door" immigration policy. "America is now drinking the bitter dregs of multiculturalism and diversity," declared the council on its website, which also displayed an essay linking 9/11 to Abraham Lincoln and America's "[sinful] religion of equality and unity."

Anti-Semitic Canards

Former Klan Imperial Wizard David Duke, who won 607,000 votes when he ran for the US Senate in 1990, trumpeted a similar message in October [2001] saying, "If the demographics of America were still the same as in the 1960s we would be absolutely secure." Duke was last seen in Moscow hawking his hate-filled autobiography, *My Awakening*, and he has been raising money to underwrite his next book, *Jewish Supremacism*. In the post-9/11 issue of his newsletter, Duke explained that "reason should tell us that even if Israeli agents were not the actual provocateurs behind the operation [on 9/11], at the very least they had prior knowledge. . . . Zionists caused the attack America endured just as surely as if they themselves had piloted those planes. It was caused by the Jewish control of the American media and Congress."

Although such anti-Semitic canards have been widely endorsed in the foreign Arab press, most Americans have rejected these and other conspiracy theories out of hand. Still, Duke and others aren't trying to reach a general audience. The anti-Jewish line of the radical right since 9/11 is aimed at the 17 percent of American adults (an estimated 35 million) who, according to a recent survey by Marttila Communications Group and Kiley & Company for the Anti-Defamation League, hold significantly anti-Semitic views—as well as the one out of five people who, as a recent Harris poll reports, blame America's support for Israel for the attacks.

Virulent Hatred

As U.S. intelligence agents strained to pick up conversations among Al Qaeda [terrorists] gloating over their September 11 [2001], success, soldiers in America's racist underground gnashed over their teeth over not having carried out the attack on "Jew York" themselves. "It's a DISGRACE that in a population of at least 150 MILLION White/Aryan Americans, we provide so FEW that are willing to do the same," bemoaned Rocky Suhayda, Nazi Party chairman from Eastpointe, Michigan. "[A] bunch of towel head/sand niggers put our great White Movement to SHAME."

Suhayda's chilling online comments, collected with other racist postings by the Southern Poverty Law Center, merely hint at the virulent hatred shared by thousands of extremists within U.S. borders. . . . Some of these people have yearned to acquire the means of biochemical warfare, and today they're openly calling for an assault.

James Ridgeway, *Village Voice*, November 6, 2001.

While it might seem counterintuitive for the radical right to be making both anti-Arab and anti-Semitic appeals, hatred of Jews and Arabs has never been mutually exclusive. After all, there have been many Holocaust deniers and other neo-Nazis who have allied themselves with the Arab cause when it comes to denouncing Jews but who still hold racist views of Arabs. And the radical right stands to gain from denouncing both groups. There are still millions of garden-variety anti-Semites, some of whom will be receptive to the message that 9/11 was a Zionist plot or the result of Jews having "too much power"—or both. Just because some Americans are seething with anti-Arab bigotry doesn't mean the radical right isn't also using September 11 to promote anti-Semitism.

Enter William Pierce, founder of the neo-Nazi National Alliance and author of the racist novel *The Turner Diaries*. In a September 22, 2001, Internet radio broadcast, the former assistant professor of physics claimed that America was attacked "because we have been letting ourselves be used to do all of Israel's dirty work in the Middle East." The National Alliance distilled this message into a flier that pictured the disintegrating towers and asked the rhetorical question, "Is Our Involvement in the Security of the Jewish State Worth This?" Beyond 9/11, Pierce is investing heavily in the skinhead music business. Although the aging neo-Nazi would much prefer listening to Wagner, he paid $250,000 in 1999 for Resistance Records, a "white power" music label that now generates about $1 million a year for his hard-core National Alliance.[1] According to Justin Massa of the Chicago-based Center for New Community, which has launched a nationwide campaign to counter neo-Nazi bands and hate music (www.turnitdown.com), "White power music has become the number one recruitment tool for organized bigots hoping to turn healthy youth rebellion into white supremacy."

The Spin of the Christian Right

In the minds of most Americans, Osama bin Laden was responsible for 9/11, but leaders of the Christian right tried to put their own self-serving spin on events. In addition to joining the conservative chorus assailing Arabs and immigration, Pat Robertson argued that the attacks occurred because America had insulted God "at the highest levels of our government" through "rampant secularism," pornography and abortion. As punishment, "God Almighty. . .lift[ed] his protection from us," declared Robertson on *The 700 Club* on September 13, [2001]. His guest that day, the Rev. Jerry Falwell, agreed: The ACLU and other godless secularists clearly were to blame. "I really believe that the pagans, and the abortionists, and the feminists, and the gays and the lesbians who are actively trying to make that an alternative lifestyle. . .all of them who have tried to secularize America. I point the finger in their face and say 'you helped this happen.'"

"Well, I totally concur," said Robertson. Both men spent the next two months trying to undo the damage to their reputations incurred by these remarks. Among other factors, the embarassment contributed to Robertson's December 5

1. William Pierce died on July 23, 2002.

[2001], resignation as director of the Christian Coalition.

Robertson and others on the Christian right have also rushed to the defense of Israel—though such support is strongly rooted in the perverse theological notion that Israel must be supported to prepare for the Second Coming of Christ, when Jew's will either convert or be destroyed.

If the hijackers of 9/11 believed they would be rewarded in heaven, so, too, did the antiabortion zealot who sent fake anthrax through the mail. The first round of hoax letters—more than 280 of them—began arriving at family planning and abortion clinics in seventeen states in the second week of October 2001 (coincidentally, the same week that staffers in the office of Senate majority leader Tom Daschle unleashed a plume of real anthrax spores when they opened an envelope sent from a fictitious fourth-grade class in Franklin Park, New Jersey). The envelopes, containing harmless white powder, were marked "Time Sensitive" and "Urgent Security Notice Enclosed," bore the return address of the US Marshals Service or the Secret Service, and included threatening messages signed by the Army of God, a well-known militant anti-abortion group. Still, it took two more weeks for the FBI to open a national investigation. And despite demands from abortion advocates and healthcare providers, Attorney General Ashcroft has yet to designate the Army of God a domestic terrorist group. . . .

Racist Patriots and Militants

Twenty years ago, the self-described Christian Patriot movement spread across rural America, recruiting thousands of bankrupt farmers with bogus rhetoric about an "International Jewish Banking Conspiracy." Those were hard times, and fearmongering speeches about the Trilateral Commission and the Federal Reserve fell on receptive ears. While organizations like the Posse Comitatus were trying to build a mass movement, racist militants associated with the underground group the Order deluded themselves into believing they could instigate a race war by robbing banks, counterfeiting money and assassinating their enemies. But rightwing criminality has always cut both ways. On the one hand, it has been used to inspire followers to take action, it has helped finance the movement and it has resulted in plenty of publicity, which these groups often crave. On the other hand, the movement's crimes often mobilize its opposition, lead to public disgust and can prompt more aggressive government surveillance and prosecution. While the violence of the Order in the 1980s inspired a generation of militant skinheads and others, the crackdown that followed pushed some hate-group leaders to explore different options, especially in the electoral arena. Organizations like the Populist Party—an offshoot of the far-right Liberty Lobby, based in Washington, DC—canvassed the radical right for contributions and candidates. Among the latter was David Duke, who ran a lackluster third-party presidential campaign as a Populist in 1988. But Duke was elected to the Louisiana State House a year later, and in 1990 he won the support of 60 percent of Louisiana's white voters in his Senate bid.

The militia movement of the early 1990s was fed not by hard times but by hard-core ideological opposition to gun control, "big government" and globalization. It was easy to parody the paranoid rants about invasions by black helicopters and blue-helmeted UN troops, but the same nationalist fears about America's waning stature in an increasingly global world were shared by millions of mainstream Americans who had nothing to do with the militias. The deaths of Branch Davidians in Waco—and of family members of hardened white supremacist Randy Weaver in Idaho—also helped fuel the militia movement at the same time as they inspired Timothy McVeigh and Terry Nichols to commit mass murder. But regardless of how many hard-core militiamen bought one or more of the myriad conspiracy theories about who was really behind the Oklahoma City bombing, the sight of nine stories of the Alfred P. Murrah building reduced to rubble, juxtaposed with regular news reports about the escapades of militia groups, doomed any hope the paramilitary right might have had for translating antigovernment sentiment into popular support. The approaching millennium and fears of Y2K offered doomsday-preaching patriots a temporary reprieve, but when nothing happened after midnight on December 31, 1999, the movement again lost recruits.

Although the radical right never reached a consensus about

supporting Pat Buchanan in the 2000 presidential race, his message of white Christian nationalism was well received by many militants. Buchanan managed to seize the Reform Party and $12.6 million in federal matching funds, even as he fared dismally on Election Day. Buchanan's recent book, *The Death of the West*, which laments the demise of white Anglo-Saxon culture (and its accompanying gene pool), enjoyed twelve weeks on the *New York Times* bestseller list.

Exploiting Racial Fears

Long before September 11, large numbers of Americans held negative views of Arabs and immigrants. One ABC News poll, conducted in 1991, found that majorities of Americans saw Arabs as "terrorists" (59 percent), "violent" (58 percent) and "religious fanatics" (56 percent). And a Gallup poll conducted two years later found that two-thirds of Americans believed that there were "too many" Arab immigrants in the United States. A *Newsweek* poll conducted immediately in the wake of 9/11 revealed that 32 percent of Americans favored putting Arabs under special surveillance like that of Japanese-Americans during World War II. Sixty-two percent of Americans disagreed, but the fact that nearly one-third supported the idea indicates the untapped potential of anti-immigrant and right-wing groups. Anti-Arab attitudes have not softened much since.

True, the radical right suffers from a lack of stable, well-funded organizations as well as a shortage of leaders, finances and organizational vehicles capable of penetrating very far into the political mainstream. But in the wake of 9/11 there are plenty of highly charged racial issues for the far right to inflame and exploit, especially when it comes to questions of immigration, racial profiling and national security. Be on the lookout, then, for more hardened underground activity as well as a concerted effort to recruit and mobilize new supporters based on fear and distrust of Arabs, immigrants, Israel and American Jews.

"Most groups in the grassroots right avoid advocates of violence like anthrax."

The Far Right Is Not a Threat

Samuel Francis

In an attempt to undermine their opponents, liberals wrongly link the grassroots right with groups that advocate violence and terrorism, columnist Samuel Francis argues in the following viewpoint. Yet the vast majority of ultra-conservatives—such as those who oppose immigration, homosexuality, and abortion—are not members of hate groups, Francis points out. Moreover, nearly all violent attacks on minorities in the past two decades were committed by individuals, not organized groups. The real threat of violence comes not from the far right but from terrorists living in America, such as the foreign-born recruits of al-Qaeda, the Islamic terrorist organization responsible for the September 11, 2001, terrorist attacks, Francis concludes.

As you read, consider the following questions:
1. According to Francis, what restrictions limited the effectiveness of the FBI in the 1970s and 1980s?
2. Which groups are part of the industry of "hate hunters," in the author's view?
3. What do "hate hunters" do to influence law enforcement and intelligence agencies, according to Francis?

Samuel Francis, "Principalities and Powers: Hate, Inc.," *Chronicles*, vol. 26, October 2002, pp. 33–34. Copyright © 2002 by *Chronicles*. Reproduced by permission of the publisher and the author.

No sooner had victory in Afghanistan by the forces of Truth, Beauty, and Global Democracy been announced and the still uncaptured and undeceased Osama bin Laden declared by President Bush to be "unimportant" (no doubt the reason the administration put a $25-million reward on his head last fall) than the top-ranking officials of the U.S. government informed the nation that terrorist attacks within the United States were a virtual certainty. On May 19, Vice President Cheney told *Meet the Press*, "The prospects of a future attack on the United States are almost certain. Not a matter of if, but when." The very next day, FBI Director Robert Mueller told a gathering of district attorneys in Washington that suicide bombings and other terrorist attacks inside the United States were "inevitable," that "there will be another terrorist attack," and "we will not be able to stop it." And the day after that, Secretary of Defense Donald Rumsfeld told a Senate committee that terrorists will "inevitably" gain control of "weapons of mass destruction" and will not hesitate to use them against us. For all the administration's chest-thumping about the glory of driving the mad mullahs of the Taliban from the field of battle, it might seem that a certain degree of skepticism about the scope and meaning of our "victory" is in order.

The officials who pronounced their solemn warnings were probably correct, and, certainly, for a nation that has insanely allowed some 30 million aliens from the most backward portions of the globe to settle here in the course of the last three decades, terrorist attacks are the least that we should expect. In a study released in May, the Center for Immigration Studies in Washington found that no fewer than 48 foreign-born radical Muslims have been implicated in terrorism in this country since 1993 and that they

> have manipulated almost every possible means of admission to the United States: Some have indeed come as students, tourists, and business travelers; others, however, have been Lawful Permanent Residents and naturalized U.S. citizens; while yet others have snuck across the border, arrived as stowaways on ships, used false passports, been granted amnesty, or been applicants for asylum.

A week or so later, *U.S. News and World Report* detailed the profiles of "more than three dozen American jihadists, many of them previously unknowns" and many of whom "are U.S. citizens, native born or naturalized," though "a fair number are African-Americans, who make up nearly one-third of the nation's Muslims."

The arrest of native-born American Jose Padilla, now known as "Abdullah al Muhajir," on charges of plotting with Al Qaeda to deploy a nuclear bomb in the United States, points to the same phenomenon, as does the estimate of terrorism expert Peter J. Brown, who says there may be as many as "1,500 to 2,000 American passport-carrying recruits who have shown up in the ranks of al Qaeda in the past decade." President Bush was right: Osama bin Laden is not particularly important, and neither is Afghanistan. What's important, and a threat to the nation, are the alien hordes that the Open Borders lobby has insisted on importing into this country through the immigration policy it has succeeded in dictating against the wishes of most Americans.

Rather belatedly, then, the administration last spring began taking steps to deal with what is now rather fetchingly known as "homeland security": not only the creation of yet another behemoth government agency at the Cabinet level, larger than any other department save the Pentagon, with a budget of $37 billion, 170,000 employees, and combining 22 existing federal agencies, but also the long-sought "unleashing" of the FBI a week or so before by the abolition of the attorney general's guidelines for domestic security and terrorism investigations. Given the magnitude of the threat as estimated by administration officials and the internal location of the threat as indicated by the figures provided, the government buildup and crackdown might seem entirely justified. In fact, however, it will do little to deal with the real and existing internal security threat but much to endanger what remains of American political freedom and dissent, especially from the ideological right.

The creation of the so-called Department of Homeland Security ought to speak for itself, and indeed, congressional criticism of the proposed department concentrated on the claim that it didn't go far enough, that it had no intelligence-gathering powers of its own, and that both the FBI and the CIA should be absorbed within it. Doing so would complete the evolution of what could only be called an "American Gestapo," an agency that would, in fact, dwarf the secret police of the German National Socialist government and approach being able to swallow the rest of the federal government itself. There is no reason whatsoever to believe that creating such an agency would improve federal counter-terrorist policies or reduce the threat of terrorism, internal or external, in any way.

It is the abolition of the attorney general's guidelines for FBI investigations, however, that are of more interest than yet another sequel to the never-ending epic of the governmental Frankenstein. Imposed in 1976 by Gerald Ford's attorney general, Edward Levi, the guidelines were intended to curb the supposed "excesses" of the Bureau of that and earlier eras (when it actually carried out essential functions of national security by spying on communists and other enemies, harassing subversives, and surveilling such known security risks as Martin Luther King, Jr.). Some of the Bureau's domestic security, activities, such as J. Edgar Hoover's personal animosity toward the Ku Klux Klan and other opponents of the "civil-rights movement," did indeed go too far, and in one case an FBI undercover agent seems to have instigated the actual murder of a "civil-rights worker"; but Hoover himself annually and publicly reported the general nature of his agency's activities to Congress, and there was a wide if somewhat vague national consensus about what he and his G-men were supposed to be doing. It was only the political triumph of the left in the wake of Watergate and the post-Vietnam era (and the flaccidity of the Republican right under such weaklings as Gerald Ford) that allowed restrictions on the Bureau (and the CIA) to be imposed at all.

The Levi guidelines effectively made it impossible for the FBI to investigate what was, in that era, the very real terrorism of the far left. The guidelines imposed what is known as a "criminal standard," under which the Bureau could not open an investigation of a group unless it knew the group was involved in or planning criminal activity. A mere rhetoric of violence, simply calling for violent overthrow of the government, assassination of public officials, or bombing public buildings, wasn't enough to justify an FBI investigation.

Of course, if the FBI knew that the members of a group

actually were planning or involved in crimes, it had no reason to *investigate* at all; it then had reason to *arrest* them. Moreover, the guidelines contained a catch-22: You couldn't investigate a group unless you knew there was criminal conduct. But you couldn't know there was criminal conduct unless you investigated. Under those guidelines, the FBI really couldn't do much at all to keep nutty groups that may have had links with terrorists or hostile foreign powers under surveillance. As a result, the FBI dropped its investigation of the Weather Underground Organization in 1979; two years later, when remnants of the Weathermen were committing a series of armored-car robberies and murders, the FBI didn't have a clue—literally. Only when a police roadblock after a robbery and brutal murder on Long Island in 1981 nabbed several Weathermen (and Weatherwomen, including the long-missing Kathy Boudin) did it become clear that real terrorism—not just ordinary robberies— was involved.

The Crusade to End "Hate"

The national press and Jewish organizations argue that we are headed down the slippery slope toward the Third Reich unless we relentlessly crusade against homophobia, sexism, and Christian intolerance. The most shocking expression of it I have encountered was a recent display at the local Barnes and Noble, sponsored by B'nai B'rith and the National Gay and Lesbian Alliance. Next to *The Diary of Anne Frank* and other holocaust-related literature were *Heather Has Two Mommies* and further instructional studies produced by the advocates of "alternative lifestyles." This reading matter, explained the accompanying poster, was essential to the crusade "to end hate right now."

Paul Gottfried, *Chronicles*, March 2001.

In that era, then, there was good reason to get rid of the guidelines, although any attempt to do so was immediately greeted with denunciations from the left (and not a few from the libertarian "right") of "fascism" and "McCarthyism." Today, however, the situation is rather different.

Today the violent, disloyal, and revolutionary left, in league with hostile foreign powers, seems to be either defunct or dying (although there are scads of Weathermen who simply vanished and have never been found, and several million dollars from the 1981 armored-car robberies has never been located), and they don't pose much of a physical danger. Why blow up the government when you essentially control it? Today, the great enemy, the great target for any renewed campaign of domestic security, is what is called "Hate."

"Hate," of course, does not necessarily mean real hatred but what the leftists who have acquired cultural hegemony in recent decades like to call "hate." Mostly, what they are talking about is merely political dissidence on the right that includes not only real "hate groups" that carry out violence against minorities (very few, if any, to my knowledge; almost all the violent incidents associated with "the right" in the last 20 years or so have been committed by individuals rather than actual groups or organizations) but groups that simply take what these days are considered to be unfashionable or "ultra-conservative" positions: opposition to immigration, support for the Confederate flag, opposition to abortion and homosexuality, support for the Second Amendment and resistance to gun control, *etc.* While the "mainstream" or "neoconservative" "right" generally avoids these issues or is actually on the other side of some of them, support for them has fallen into the hands of largely grassroots groups that, by definition, lie outside the mainstream created by the dominant left-right political establishment.

One of the major tactics of the political left in recent years has been to destroy this grassroots opposition to some of its most cherished goals by demonizing it as "hate" and "linking" it to groups that actually do advocate or, at least, play with violence. In fact, very little connection exists, and most groups in the grassroots right avoid advocates of violence like anthrax. Nevertheless, there is an entire industry of "hate hunters" like the Southern Poverty Law Center of Morris Dees, the Anti-Defamation League of B'nai B'rith, and similar groups that specialize in raising vast sums of money by claiming that "hate groups" are about to unleash violence against the government, Jews, liberals, ethnic groups, abortionists, homosexuals, etc. Their "research" is usually transparently biased if not factually worthless, and their own political orientation is obvious. A few years ago, I heard a lecture by Mark Potok, publications director of the Southern Poverty Law Center, in which he alleged that religious-right leaders Pat Robertson and Gary Bauer had "provided the moral atmosphere" for the murder of homosexual Matthew Shepard in Wyoming—a claim that is as preposterous as it is ideologically driven. As investigator Laird Wilcox (who has researched the so-called "watchdog" groups extensively) has written,

> Activists with a hidden radical agenda find antiracist organizations very amenable to manipulation. . . . In rational terms, class struggle Marxism-Leninism is a hard sell. However, when it is reframed as anti-racism and anti-fascism, much of the onus is gone.

Professional hate-hunters such as Mr. Potok and his ilk influence federal, state, and local law-enforcement agencies. Their "experts" often testify in trials and provide seminars for law-enforcement and intelligence agencies on the "real threats" to national security, and the cops and bureaucrats whom they brief often don't know any better. Faced with demands from the public and their superiors to "stop terrorism" and get information on groups and individuals too obscure for most media to cover, they eagerly gobble up the propaganda masked as "research" or "intelligence" that the hate industry feeds them. In 1999, the industry helped to produce a report for the FBI itself warning of massive right-wing violence on the eve of the turn of the millennium. There was, of course, no such violence. The same sources were largely responsible for the similar black-church arson hoax of 1996—there were few such acts of arson that were racially motivated.

There is, of course, a need for the federal government to investigate real domestic-security threats, and the thousands of aliens who represent such a threat should be and probably are at the top of the Bureau's list these days. But there will come a day when the new masters of the federal leviathan will steer its attention toward other groups that represent no threat to the nation at all and whose only offense is their perfectly legal support for perfectly legal causes that just happen to jeopardize the total power for which the left has long reached and which it now—thanks to mass immigration and the Bush administration—nearly has within its grasp.

> *"Music is the common thread that links neo-Nazi skinheads, serving as a source of entertainment, a propaganda tool and a weapon to incite violence."*

White Power Musicians Promote Hate and Violence

John M. Cotter

Neo-Nazi skinheads use white power rock and roll as a propaganda tool to attract recruits and incite violence, argues John M. Cotter in the following viewpoint. White power music promotes hatred by highlighting alleged threats to "Aryan" culture from Jews, minorities, immigrants, liberals, homosexuals, and criminals, Cotter points out. White power song lyrics also glorify aggression, war, and sacrifice—characteristics that neo-Nazis wish to emphasize as they prepare for an apocalyptic battle between whites and nonwhites. Contrary to some predictions, neo-Nazi skinheads will continue to present a hate-crimes threat due to the continuing spread of racist propaganda through music. Cotter was a Ph.D. student in the Department of Political Science at the University of Kentucky when he wrote this essay.

As you read, consider the following questions:

1. According to Cotter, what are some of the theories on the appeal of the neo-Nazi skinhead culture?
2. When and where did the skinhead subculture originate? How did the subculture evolve, according to the author?
3. In Cotter's opinion, why are first- and second-generation skinheads likely to present "the greatest danger"?

John M. Cotter, "Sounds of Hate: White Power Rock and Roll and the Neo-Nazi Skinhead Subculture," *Terrorism and Political Violence*, vol. 11, Summer 1999, pp. 111–36. Copyright © 2002 by Frank Cass & Company, Ltd. Reproduced by permission.

S ince the 1980s, . . . the West has witnessed a resurgence in the organization and appeal of right-wing extremist groups. Differentiated by their affinity for authoritarian forms of government and exclusive nationalism, the far right has found new life in Eastern Europe as well, partially filling an ideological void left after the demise of the Soviet Union.

This rise of the right takes two general forms. The first, which has received the most attention from scholars, is the increased electoral appeal of so-called 'radical right-wing parties', such as Jean-Marie Le Pen's *Front National* in France, or Austria's Freedom Party led by Jörg Haider. These parties combine anti-immigrant rhetoric with a commitment to free-market capitalism to create an unusual political platform that has won them surprising support in several European democracies. So far, most of Europe's radical right-wing parties have shown a commitment to working within the institutional framework of democracy, and in the process, have distanced themselves from the use of violence against their opponents.

The same may not be said of the second manifestation of the rise of the right—the increase in the number and activity of militant neo-Nazi organizations and violent youth subcultures, which have received less attention from social scientists. Unlike the radical right-wing parties, organizations on the extreme right rarely, if ever, run for elective office. Instead, drawing on the ideology of Nazism, they reject competitive liberal democratic government and consider themselves 'warriors', fighting against a conspiracy of enemies to restore ethnic or racial purity to their homelands. Further, the more militant extreme right does not dismiss the use of violence for political purposes. Instead, violence is perfectly justified in, or even natural to, their cause of racially cleansing society and achieving a state that seeks to maintain this differentiation between groups. Most of the time the extreme right is waging a propaganda war—seeking to warn others about the decline of their racial group. Increasingly, however, terrorism and less systematic 'terroristic violence', such as assaults, harassment and vandalism, have been used to drive out foreigners, gain funds to continue their activities or attack the state which has betrayed their interests.

Neo-Nazi Skinheads

This essay concerns one subgroup of this revived network of militant neo-Nazi organizations that has been labeled 'terrorist youth subcultures', or skinheads and their associates. Despite coverage of skinheads' extensive record of violence by the media and 'watchdog' organizations of the far right, social scientists have paid only limited attention to this subculture that has been called 'the most violent of all white supremacy groups'. Hypotheses on the origins and appeal of the skinhead subculture and the violence associated with it are numerous, and to a certain extent, overlapping. Some argue that skinheads are involved in a 'youthful rebellion' against the norms of post-industrial society and their parents. Others claim skinheads are responding to modern economic uncertainties, caused by an increase in the amount of immigration to Western states in general. Finally, skinheads are said to be alienated and isolated young people seeking to recover a sense of community and personal identity. Unfortunately, in the absence of systematic study of the skinhead subculture, there is a lingering 'difficulty of separating confirmed knowledge from theoretical speculation', [according to researcher Christopher T. Husbands]. Implicit in some of the explanations, is the belief that this diffuse and violent youth movement will slowly wither away in appeal and significance, as other youth styles have done in the past.

Despite the predictions and hopes among researchers and government officials of an imminent demise of the skinhead subculture, the movement continues to attract an estimated 70,000 members in 33 countries. Regardless of the country in question, skinheads continue to be responsible for numerous instances of hate crime ranging from intimidation to murder. This leads to several questions. Why has this neo-Nazi subculture, that has its origins in 1970s Great Britain, been so durable? What is responsible for its diffusion and appeal to numerous other settings? And perhaps most importantly, why are skinheads so violent?

The answer to these questions lies, in part, with the development and distribution of one critically important aspect of the skinhead lifestyle—white power rock and roll music. It is almost universally accepted that music is the common thread that links neo-Nazi skinheads, serving as a source of entertainment, a propaganda tool and a weapon to incite violence. Despite this acknowledgement that skinhead music is important in perpetuating the subculture, this aspect of the skinhead phenomena has been underrated and has virtually escaped systematic analysis. This essay is an attempt to rectify this oversight by explicitly focusing on the role white power rock and roll music has played in the development, diffusion, and perpetuation of the skinhead subculture and the violence that is so ingrained within it. . . .

Skinheads, the National Front, and Ian Stuart

The skinhead subculture traces its origins back to the tough working-class neighborhoods of East London where it evolved from other youth styles during the 1960s. This style that celebrated male toughness and British working-class identity had nearly disappeared as of the late 1970s, only to experience a 'rebirth' sparked by the influence of 'punk' rock and its anti-social behavior. The sound associated with this resurgence in skinhead activity was a variant of punk rock called British *Oi!* music, which combined hard and steady rock and roll music with lyrics expressing working-class frustration and exalting male camaraderie. By the early 1980s a substantial proportion of skinheads had become affiliated with British right-wing extremist organizations, such as the National Front [NF] and British Movement, that were experiencing a similar resurgence during a period of economic downturn and increased immigration to the United Kingdom from Third World countries. From the ranks of the National Front emerged Ian Stuart, whose career as a musician and organizer of skinheads and their sympathizers is largely responsible for the development and diffusion of the modern neo-Nazi skinhead subculture and white power rock and roll. . . .

Skinheads' association with violence, disdain for the political establishment and vision of a declining working-class fueled by increasing resentment of Third World immigrants, made them increasingly attractive to right-wing extremist organizations in Great Britain. Shortly following the revival of the skinhead subculture, the NF realized their potential to become soldiers for the similarly revitalized British far right in their own brand of 'street politics'. In the late 1970s, the NF politicized a large segment of the skinhead scene with neo-Nazi ideology that appealed to their frustration with Britain's economic and political situation, isolating immigrants and Jewish conspirators as the culprits of the British working-class decline.

The Young National Front (YNF) was established at the party's Annual General Meeting in October 1977 and quickly grew in size, using a variety of appeals including seminars on British Nationalist ideology, anti-immigrant demonstrations and soccer tournaments, all of which were advertised in the organization's newsletter titled *Bulldog*. However, the most influential and lucrative medium used to infuse right-wing extremist ideology into their new youthful allies was music. The man charged with making this connection between right-wing extremist ideology and the skinhead subculture was Ian Stuart, who with his band Skrewdriver, is largely responsible for inventing white power rock and roll and using it to construct today's informal international skinhead network. . . .

Through the 1980s and continuing into the 1990s, right up to his death in an automobile accident in 1993, Ian Stuart remained a fixture in the neo-Nazi skinhead movement. But the contemporary neo-Nazi skinhead movement is no longer confined to several countries in northwestern Europe, with a handful of bands and a few distributors. Instead, the current international skinhead subculture has spread to over 30 countries, with more than 100 white power bands and a consistently growing number of transnational distributors of white power rock and roll—all contributing to the formation of hundreds of autonomous skinhead gangs from Europe, to the Americas and to Australia. Regardless of the country or individual gang in question, white power rock and roll and violence are constants. Within this time period, neo-Nazi skinheads have deservedly gained a reputation as the most consistently violent element of the diverse right-wing extremist constellation.

Virtually every discussion of neo-Nazi skinheads to date at least mentions the importance of white power rock and roll in the spread of the subculture over the last two decades, as well as the increased violence associated with the growth of skinhead organization and activity. Analysts, whether reporters or social scientists, have tended to depict skinheads as violent racist gangs who are enraged by the hard and steady beats of *Oi!* music accompanied by lyrics laced with profanity and racial epithets directed toward minority groups. Although this characterization is true to a certain extent, it does not capture the complexity of the white power rock and roll industry. First, white power rock and roll is not universally within the bounds of what may be referred to as *Oi!* music. In fact, white power rock and roll has several different styles of music ranging from standard rock and roll, 'heavy metal', punk/*Oi!*, soft ballads and even a bizarre mutation of bluegrass/country music dubbed 'psycho-billy'.

Second, and more importantly, white power rock and roll is more ideologically sophisticated than the above characterization implies. Many songs are indeed invectives against minority groups. However, white power rock and roll lyrics convey other themes associated with right-wing extremist ideology, such as the notion of a global Jewish conspiracy against the white race, the complicity of state governments in this plot and a belief in the inevitability of a brutal war between races in which the warriors of the Aryan race will eventually emerge victorious. Third, this simple characterization tends to overlook the potential independent role of white power rock and roll in spreading the skinhead subculture, as well as consistently inciting violent behavior. Evidence from Mark S. Hamm's groundbreaking criminological study of American skinheads indicates that white power rock and roll is the preferred music of skinheads who have engaged in violent behavior. Not all listeners of white power rock and roll engage in violence, but prolonged exposure to this form of racist propaganda is likely to contribute to skinhead violence.

In general, the ideology found in neo-Nazi skinhead music fits rather well into themes consistently found in contemporary right-wing extremist rhetoric, including: hatred toward outgroups, antisemitic conspiracy theories, chauvinistic nationalism and a disregard for conventional political behavior. . . .

Hatred for Outgroups

The belief most associated with right-wing extremist groups, especially neo-Nazi skinheads, is hatred for outgroups. This is what may be called an 'ideology of inequality' that rigidly separates people according to those who 'belong' and those who do not. White power rock and roll demonstrates that this hatred is directed at multiple minority groups. One of the more common and convenient groups for verbal and physical attacks is unwanted immigrants and refugees. Skinheads object to the increased number of 'foreigners' for two interrelated reasons. First is a material objection, where immigrants are accused of stealing increasingly scarce jobs, government transfers or housing from the hard-working native white populations, considered the legitimate consumers of these benefits the Western world has to offer. The excerpts from two songs, one by Ian Stuart's alternative band White Diamond and Australia's Fortress express anti-foreigner sentiment so common among today's far right milieu, especially skinheads:

> They all come here from distant lands
> Well it seems to me that it has all been planned
> What are they looking for
> They have seen the open door
> Not enough for our own folk
> So coming here is just a joke
>
> Refugee, you're not fooling me
> Refugee, you just want a jobs monopoly
>
> We got no money, we got no home
> Yet they're arriving in their droves
> If violence happens that's a shame
> Politicians and their games
> Everyone chose to fill their hand
> What about the people of our own land[1]

• • • • •

> Get out of my country . . .
> Get out, we don't want you around
> Get out, is what the people shout
> Get out, get out of my sight
> Get out, parasite

1. White Diamond, "Refugee," *The Power and the Glory*, 1992.

Victory of an alien government
Don't recognize their law
It's time to close the flood gates
It's time to shut the door

Repatriate, ship them out, send the bastards back
If they don't fucking like it, they'll be in body bags[2]

Foreigners are only part of a diverse collective seen as responsible for the current decline of Western nations. Other vilified groups include anti-racists, Marxists, liberal politicians, homosexuals and criminal elements. These forces combine to facilitate the entry of 'alien' elements that destroy the cultural purity of the national group or white race, as well as contribute to the current state of moral decadence and cultural decay common to all Western states. Any of these groups are potential targets for attack, as skinheads contend that they are charged with expelling and keeping out these inferior elements and their traitorous allies within the white race itself. Skinheads' solution to problems concerning law and order and cultural decline is their own special brand of 'street justice' with harsh penalties for offenders, as seen in the lyrics of 'Simple Man' from the well-known British group No Remorse:

They tell our kids to just say 'No'
And then some out of touch Judge
Lets a drug-pusher go
He slaps him on the wrist
And turns him back out on the Town
But if I had my way with people selling dope
I'd take a big, tall tree
And a short piece of rope
I'd hang 'em up high
And let 'em swing 'till the sun goes down . . .

As far as I'm concerned
There ain't no excuse
For the raping and killing
And the child abuse
I've got a way
To put an end to all those things
You take that scum
And put a bullet in their heads
Or hang 'em from a tree

2. Fortress, "Parasite," *Fortress*, 1992.

Until they drop down dead
And let them be an example
To all the rest[3]

Antisemitism and Conspiracy Theories

Antisemitism and the belief in the threat of Jewish world domination are not new to the far right. However, contemporary right-wing extremist 'ZOG [Zionist Occupation Government] discourse' differs from its predecessors in two ways. First, it argues that the anti-white conspiracy is much more elaborate and widespread than previously believed, reaching the highest levels of Western governments. Therefore, Jews and their collaborators are the forces behind the threat to white civilization, making other minorities a lesser concern. Second, it argues that the conspirators are dangerously close to achieving their ultimate objectives of global Jewish domination *and* the destruction of the white race, thus necessitating drastic measures in response and direct confrontation with governmental authorities.

The idea of ZOG, which stands for Zionist Occupation Government, developed in the 1970s American white supremacist constellation and has since become influential in most violent right-wing extremist circles throughout the West, including neo-Nazi skinheads. As argued, all the ills that plague Western societies are the work of ZOG, this includes not only Jews, but also traitors within the white race such as the media, intellectuals, police and politicians. . . .

For all their violent rhetoric, right-wing extremists in general are mostly involved in propaganda efforts to reveal the hidden threats faced by the white race. Neo-Nazi skinheads are the exception to this rule, earning a reputation for being the most violent of all right-wing extremist groups. White power rock and roll provides insight into this subculture that not only legitimizes violence, but also celebrates it by urging others to join the cause in a final mythical battle against the forces of evil, a battle fought by brave and noble heroes of the white race. Herein lies the largest contradiction in skinhead music—despite the grave situation and powerful forces allied

3. No Remorse, "Simple Man," *Under the Gods*, 1994.

133

against them, the struggle goes on and one day whites will rise up and defeat ZOG 'against all odds'.

"Do Something"

White power rock and roll serves as a rallying cry to skinheads and the broader right-wing extremist movement. It appeals to whites' racial loyalty, urging them to acknowledge the threats to their kinfolk, and then stand up against their enemies. Skinheads have contempt not only for anti-racists who fight for the 'wrong' side, but also for those who do nothing, sometimes referred to as 'middle-class fools', who sit on the fence between the two opposing camps and ignore the decline of their nation and race. The following song by the most notorious American skinhead band, called Bound for Glory, asks whites to do the right thing and join the nationalist cause:

> What will it take to set yourself free
> One more mistake before you finally see
> That things aren't really all that they're cracked up to be
> As the government condemns white people like you and me
>
> You find it hard to believe the things I say
> These things go on everyday
> Open your eyes and you will see
> Join the fight and set yourself free
>
> You see I was a believer in what was called the American way
> But now times have changed and because I'm white there's a
>   price to pay
> It's a price so great, it's so hard to conceive
> But once you have seen, then you will believe
>
> Listen to my words for I speak the truth
> Now look around and you will see my proof
> Can you not see what's right under your nose
> Or do you just turn your back when the wind starts to blow
> Can you not hear the thunder of the storm
> Or do you just fear the gods of war
> Do you not feel racial loyalty
> Can you not taste white victory[4]

The apocalyptic visions of ZOG discourse eventually culminate in a final battle to end all history in which the white race emerges victorious over the forces of evil, and then ex-

---

4. Bound for Glory, "Set Yourself Free," *Over the Top*, 1992.

acts revenge upon non-whites and race traitors for the part they played in the plot to destroy white people and their culture. White power rock and roll is full of references to this final battle. Skinheads consider themselves 'white warriors' who will lead the chosen race into this impending battle. It emphasizes such values as loyalty, honor and bravery in the construction of this 'warrior' culture, where the soldiers will 'either win or die'. . . .

The neo-Nazi skinhead movement is now very much an international network. Unlike many previous attempts by the far right to co-ordinate strategy across states, skinheads are in a league by themselves in terms of developing these transnational links, although the extent of this cooperation is unclear. Many white power rock and roll songs celebrate bands travelling to various countries to do . . . concerts, promoting the skinhead ideology and lifestyle throughout the West. Their efforts are supported by an international network of skinhead music and magazine distributors that makes this propaganda readily available to any one who may be interested. . . .

Although the skinhead subculture is likely to be around for some time to come, the threat posed by these groups is more to public order and minority groups, rather than any sort of serious threat to any Western government. Despite the anti-government rhetoric, skinheads are much more 'opportunistic' attackers, who are likely to prey on more vulnerable targets, such as immigrants and homosexuals. The weapons of choice are rather crude—fists, boots, and baseball bats, instead of planned bombings of governmental institutions. As several more traditional right-wing extremist organizations have learned, skinheads lack the organizational structure for sustained action against enemies. Skinheads do have international contacts, but skinhead groups are largely autonomous gangs of teenagers and a few young men more interested in drinking beer and listening to white power rock and roll. Unfortunately, this is the most likely recipe for continuing problems with skinhead hate crime. The greatest danger may arise from first- and second-generation skinheads. These experienced propagandists could potentially form more politically effective organizations and perpetrate more sustained, large-scale acts of violence.

"*[White power] music cults . . . are the one organized means today of fostering racial consciousness in young whites.*"

White Power Musicians Promote Positive Social Values

Eric Owens

In the following viewpoint Eric Owens contends that white power bands constitute a growing musical subculture that promotes patriotism, national identity, and racial pride among whites. While some fans of white power music are simply engaging in adolescent rebellion, many middle-class teen listeners are exposed to ideas that will make them more effective as racial leaders when they become adults, Owens claims. The music encourages abstinence from drugs and promotes respect for women, children, and the elderly, the author maintains. Owens, a fan of white power music and the skinhead movement, is a Los Angeles–based Celtic folk musician and poet.

As you read, consider the following questions:
1. How has the skinhead movement developed since the late 1960s, according to Owens?
2. According to the author, what is the nature of Black Metal music?
3. How have today's media and music industries "turned morality on its head," in Owens' opinion?

Eric Owens, "The New Nationalist Music," *American Renaissance*, vol. 11, November 2000, pp. 1, 3–5. Copyright © 2000 by *American Renaissance*. Reproduced by permission.

P opular music has had a heavy, leftist overlay since at least the 1950s. Pete Seeger, Joan Baez, and Bob Dylan made protest a central part of their message, and performers who are not as explicitly political continue to give popular music an unmistakably lefty slant. Like Hollywood, the recording industry has had a deliberately corrosive effect on every sentiment and tradition healthy nationalism requires. This is still true for most commercially successful performers but there is a growing musical subculture that reflects something entirely different: a resurgence of patriotism, national identity, and even racial consciousness. The mainstream media and the music press have carefully avoided publicizing this trend, but it is growing so quickly below ground that it cannot help occasionally breaking the surface.

What kind of music is this? Who are the performers? Is this just adolescent rebellion or do white power bands reflect real racial commitment? Most people have heard about skinheads but very few know about Apocalyptic Folk, NR, or Black Metal music. I have been part of this movement myself—first as a fan, later as an active performer—and believe I can report with some authority on a phenomenon nonparticipants are not likely to understand.

The Skinhead Movement

The skinhead movement began in England in the late 1960s when young people emerging from the Mod (short for Modern) youth culture followed the lead of rock groups such as *The Who*, and wore Mod clothing draped in the Union Jack. Skinheads took most of the Mod style—Doctor Marten boots, short hair cuts, patriotism, a penchant for scooters, loud music, and violence—and carried it even further.

Throughout the late 1960s and early 1970s the skinheads were, for the most part, non-ideological toughs, known for football hooliganism (rioting at soccer games) and Paki-bashing (beating up Pakistani or Indian immigrants). Among the first skinhead bands were *Slade* and *Dexy's Midnight Runners*, the latter to become known for their international hit "C'mon Eileen."

By the mid- to late 1970s the skinheads were beginning to become politicized, and were welcomed by the Young National Front, the official youth wing of the National Front, which started enthusiastically promoting skinhead music. By the 1980s the term skinhead was firmly associated with nationalist groups like the National Front and the British National Party. There is still some association between skinheads and the British National Party, but the decline of the once-powerful National Front was due, at least in part, to a falling out with the musicians, who had been some of the party's best youth recruiters.

It was during this period of political activism that a new skinhead-specific music movement took shape. This movement was called Oi! which was the Cockney word for "Hey!" and was a kind of white working-class battle cry for musically-oriented skinheads. It was by means of this music that skinhead politics went international. Thus, through the 1980s and 1990s, the movement was no longer associated specifically with England, but with disaffected white youth worldwide. By the 1990s, Oi! had largely faded in favor of even more racially charged music styles such as RAC (Rock Against Communism/Capitalism) and Hate Core (the latter being mostly an American phenomenon.) The most popular skinhead bands today are *Skrewdriver*, (England) *Brutal Attack*, (England) and *Bound for Glory* (USA).

Apocalyptic Folk

Another less well known but highly influential development of the early 1980s National Front-era of British-turned-pan-European music is what is called Apocalyptic Folk. This movement draws less aggressive and often more intellectual audiences, and grew up around a little-known London-based punk band called *Crisis*. Tony Wakeford, who had left *Crisis* to form a National Front band called *Above the Ruins*, rejoined *Crisis* bandmate Douglas Pearce in 1981. The group changed its name to *Death in June*, began to dabble in openly Nazi imagery, and started a movement.

Death in June began recording songs about the catastrophic effects of the Second World War on Europe and the decline of Western Civilization. Songs like "Death of the West" and "We Drive East" lamented the devastating conflict between Russia and Germany that ended the war, and the lack of honor, discipline, and high standards in modern European institutions. It is highly reflective music, mixing modern and medieval folk with more modern electronic sounds.

Besides *Death in June*, the biggest bands in this genre are *Sol Invictus* (Latin for Unconquerable Sun, a name for the Persian God Mithras revered by Roman soldiers), and *Strength Through Joy* (Ireland). *Death in June* and *Strength Through Joy* recently drew a crowd of 600 at the historic El Rey Theater in Los Angeles, to the dismay of the media and despite leftist threats.

NR and Black Metal

A more recent form of music has sprung up around the French National Front. It is called NR music (short for *Nationale révolutionaire*). While its roots are in the Italian right's Alternative Music from the 1970s, it has really begun anew in France with the help of National Front radio programs such as "Radio Courtoisie." These bands avoid overtly racial themes, preferring to concentrate on the French Nationalist struggle. This music, also known as *Rock identitaire* (Identity Rock) often has a more pop-rock sound. These groups often work French medieval songs into their sets, a practice common in National Romantic movements the world over. The leading bands of this type are *Ile de France*, *Vae Victus*, and *In Memoriam*.

Yet another genre that has surfaced more recently is Black Metal. As its name suggests, it evolved from Heavy Metal. This movement didn't really take off until the 1990s, and has just begun to go global, but is now one of the fastest growing underground music movements. From the beginning, Black Metal was a backlash against mainstream music. It sneered at the mainstream music industry's watered down, effeminate rock musicians, and its performers tried to put a violent manliness and aggression back into rock music.

When Black Metal began in Norway it was openly Satanic, but has matured over the past several years. It is no longer so concerned with shock value, and has developed an ideology that has taken a hard turn to the right. Beginning with the bands *Burzum* (its name is a made-up word from the writings of J.R.R. Tolkein and signifies eternal darkness) and *Dark Throne*, the movement has traded in much of its alarming Satanism for aggressive nationalism, racial consciousness, and a celebration of Norse culture.

Like the Apocalyptic Folk bands, it is now quite common for Black Metal bands to include traditional folk songs on their albums. The cover art on their CDs is of traditional statues, artifacts, and nature scenes from the native countryside. Varg Vikarness, lead singer of *Burzum* has been chided by the music press for his unabashed racial statements, and violent nationalistic rhetoric.

Aside from ideology, an important development in this music has been its turn towards a medieval folk sound. One leading band, *Ulver*, known for fast, aggressive guitar and unearthly shrieking vocals, recently released a completely acoustic CD with medieval chorus, flutes, and classical guitar, in an amazing show of virtuosity that rivals any classical CD.

Storm, a group that broke away from *Dark Throne*, describes itself in its premier CD as National Romantic Music. This CD celebrates the glory of Norway and of Norse culture, including proud chants of "Hail Norway!" in its own brand of neo-traditional, folk-influenced, heavy-metal music. Half the songs are Norwegian folk tunes, played electrically and aggressively. This has been a very influential CD, with new bands such as Sweden's *Vintersorg* imitating this medieval-operatic heavy-metal style. The leading racial Black Metal bands are *Graveland, Veles*, and *Gontyna Kry*.

A Media Blacklist

While MTV would lead us to believe that young people want nothing but self-indulgence, tens of thousands of aggressively patriotic and racially conscious CDs are sold every year on independent record labels—without any mainstream publicity. Some of these sentiments have occasionally appeared above-ground.

Until just a few years ago, the Englishman, known only by his performing name "Morissey" and former front man of *The Smiths*, was topping charts all over the world. That was until the 1992 release of possibly his best-produced, most well thought out and musically advanced CD to date, "Your Arsenal." On this CD Morissey voiced concern for the future of his country with songs like "National Front Disco," and there are clearly nationalist sentiments throughout the album. The same British press that used to fawn over him quickly dubbed him a fascist and consigned him to worldwide obscurity.

Some may remember the Swedish group *Ace of Base* whose CD "The Sign," released in 1994, was the number-one selling album in the world. At the height of its popularity, with multiple hits to its credit, it came out that founding member Ulf Eckberg had a history as a racial activist in Sweden. While Madonna, and even nonentities like Chef continue to churn out uninspiring CDs for decades and get endless air play, a racially-conscious past guarantees any musician, no matter how talented, a one-CD career.

White Nationalist Lyrics

They're making the last film, they say it's the best,
And we all helped make it. It's called the Death of the West.
The kids from Fame will all be there, free Coca-Cola for you,
and all the monkeys from the zoo. Will there be extras, too?
A star is rising in our northern sky,
And on it we're crucified.
A chain of gold is wrapped around this world.
We're ruled by those who lie.
"Death of the West," Death in June

We will never hide from our obligation.
We will lay down our lives for our race and nation.
The red, white and the blue is flying overhead.
With true undying loyalty to victory we are led.
"Red, White and Blue," Brutal Attack

Quoted in *American Renaissance*, November 2000.

The rock group *Ultima Thule* from Sweden recently had a number-one hit on the Swedish charts, by electrifying and performing an Oi! version of the Swedish national anthem, "Du Gamla Du Frig." This chart-topper got Swedish youth tapping their toes to their national anthem and brought the Swedish flag and the Thor's Hammer pendant back into vogue until a smear-by-association campaign ended a short-lived but highly successful musical career. Critics discovered that *Ultima Thule* used to be on a white power record label from Germany called Rock-O-Rama, and had appeared on a white power compilation called "No Surrender!" along with British National Front bands such as *Skrewdriver, Brutal Attack*, and *Above the Ruins*. On their own albums *Ultima Thule* had never mentioned non-whites or used racial slurs.

The German group *Böhse Onkelz* (the Evil Uncles) hit number two on the German charts, and suddenly disappeared from view just like Morissey, *Ace of Base*, and *Ultima Thule* after the discovery of similar past associations. In the United States as well, Time Warner dropped the heavy metal band *Morbid Angel* shortly after the lead singer expressed certain views publicly.

A couple of fairly mainstream American heavy metal bands have narrowly escaped the media blacklist, largely because they've not quite reached superstar status. *Pantera*, possibly one of the biggest and longest-running heavy metal bands in America got into trouble when singer Phil Anselmo sported a T-shirt emblazoned with the three-pronged symbol of the South African Afrikaner Resistance Movement during an MTV interview. Mr. Anselmo also went on a couple of racial tirades from stage while on tour, but with a lot of back peddling he was able to save his career.

A group called *Type O-Negative*, has been made to answer a lot of questions about some extremely racially provocative songs they recorded previously under the name *Carnivore*. Unlike most bands, *Type O-Negative* offered no apologies and still enjoys as much success as its talents merit.

Finally, the old standby, Ted Nugent, hardly a representative of any New Right youth movement, was recently threatened by the League of United Latin American Citizens for declaring that anyone in America who doesn't speak English should leave. Mr. Nugent also made no apologies.

Not so lucky was the well-known heavy metal performer Glen Danzig. He expressed racial views publicly in magazine interviews, and even went so far as to record a song called "White Devil Rise!," which he later declined to release on CD. He was dropped from American Records shortly afterwards.

Thugs or Thinkers?

So what do we have here: a bunch of drunken thugs out to shock their parents or a thriving underground of racially-conscious young people making and listening to their own brand of exploratory music? Both, really. Something people must understand about these movements is that they *are* meant to shock. They are rebellions and draw rebellious young people. Many of their followers will never straighten out their lives no matter what kind of music they like. They were corrupted by MTV, bad parents, and a miserable public school system long before our music reached them. We can't expect more from the average skinhead than we can from the average white American of any kind.

The importance of these movements is that they offer ideas to many middle-class whites who may simply be passing through a period of teenage rebellion—ideas to which they might not otherwise be exposed. I myself was brought into racial consciousness through the skinhead movement and through music in particular. When today's teenagers go on to college or a career many will hold on to the ideas they picked up during their rebellious youth. Just as the corrupt ideology of the drug-filled hippie and communist movements of the 1960s did not fade away, but instead moved quietly into positions of power, one can already distinguish the rise of an intellectual and successful youth elite in the racial movement in America. These are not people who would have joined the Klan in the 1960s or 1970s, and I believe they will be able to give far better racial leadership than they ever received.

There are also benefits for the more mediocre fans who will never amount to much. They learn to take pride in their race, not to miscegenate, not to take drugs (though there is much drinking of alcohol), and not to practice abortion. Outsiders have no idea how militantly the overwhelming majority of skinheads follow these rules. So, while these music cults may not be Ph.D. training camps, they are the one organized means today of fostering racial consciousness in young whites. For the worst among them, it also offers a life without drugs, and for those who will be more successful it lays the groundwork for a racial worldview that will guide them through life. These young people have a fierce and troubled appearance, but ideologically they are much better off than the average teenager.

However unpleasant much of this music may sound to the older generations, it reaches the MTV generation in a way that books do not. It is all very well for their racially conscious elders to write carefully-footnoted research papers about immigration or IQ, but they have been doing this for years with few results.

The Appeal of the New Music

Even its most hostile detractors must recognize the powerful appeal of this new music. It has become widespread despite the fact that in Europe and Canada it is illegal to express certain racial ideas, and you can get fines and jail sentences for possession of these CDs. In Germany, France, and many other European countries, white power CDs are treated as contraband, just like drugs. Customs officials confiscate packages with addresses from known white power distributors or directed to suspected European distributors. Police routinely raid the homes of young people they think are selling these CDs. People caught with what is judged to be a commercial quantity get fines up to the equivalent of $10,000 for the first offense, and may be jailed at the court's discretion. Young people will not take risks of this kind to distribute books by Philippe Rushton or Arthur Jensen.

The older generation complains about the biased media but the skinheads and other youth cults have succeeded where their elders have failed: They have created *their own* media. With glossy color magazines like *Resistance* and slickly packaged, well produced recordings, they have completely cut the mainstream music industry out of the picture. So, while we complain about the state of our media, and continue to give money to Time Warner they give a large amount of their entertainment budget to a pro-white industry owned by pro-white organizations.

The entertainment industry is profitable. Because the mainstream media will not touch white racial consciousness, it means that this important source of funds stays entirely within our movement. For whatever it's worth, the Anti-Defamation League's estimate of the annual revenues of Resistance Records is one million dollars. And Resistance is just one of many magazines and record labels around the world.

Today's huge media corporations promote black performers who encourage drug-taking, violent abuse of women, murder, and hatred of whites while they vilify any white who dares sing about love of country and culture, or respect for veterans, the elderly, women, family, children, hard work, and racial heritage. The media and the music industry have succeeded in turning morality on its head. Racially-conscious music could help set things straight again.

Periodical Bibliography

The following articles have been selected to supplement the diverse views presented in this chapter.

Chip Berlet "Hard Times on the Hard Right," *Public Eye*, Spring 2002.

Kirsten Betsworth and Molly M. Ginty "Legacy of Hate: After Seven Long Years, I Finally Left My Husband and His Racist White Pride Group," *Good Housekeeping*, July 2001.

Warren Cannon and Angie Cohen "The Church of the Almighty White Man," *U.S. News & World Report*, July 19, 1999.

Adam Cohen "All You Need Is Hate: White-Power Music Is Thriving Abroad—and Also in the U.S.," *Time*, September 15, 2001.

Michelle Cottle "Washington Diarist: White Hope," *New Republic*, December 3, 2001.

Peter L. DeGroote "White Supremacists Cloak Bigotry in Theology," *Christian Social Action*, March/April 2001.

Samuel Francis "Principalities and Powers: The New Meaning of 'Racism,'" *Chronicles*, June 2001.

Bob Herbert "When Hate Sees an Opening," *New York Times*, January 17, 2000.

Christopher Hewitt "The Political Context of Terrorism in America: Ignoring Extremists or Pandering to Them?" *Terrorism and Political Violence*, Autumn/Winter 2000.

David E. Kaplan, Lucian Kim, and Douglas Pasternak "Nazism's New Global Threat," *U.S. News & World Report*, September 25, 2000.

Nicholas D. Kristof "Hate, American Style," *New York Times*, August 30, 2002.

Robert Stacy McCain "Hate Debate," *Insight*, June 19, 2000.

Kim Murphy "Behind All the Noise of Hate Music," *Los Angeles Times*, March 30, 2000.

James Ridgeway "Osama's New Recruits," *Village Voice*, November 6, 2001.

Sally Satel "Badness or Madness?" *Los Angeles Times*, August 15, 1999.

CHAPTER 4

How Should Society Respond to Hate Groups?

Chapter Preface

In a democratic society that supports the right to freedom of expression, responding to threats and actions perpetrated by hate groups is a delicate balancing act. American legislators and judges, for example, must determine whether seemingly racially intimidating behavior—such as burning crosses or displaying swastikas—constitutes a crime or a form of protected speech.

Recent Supreme Court cases regarding "expressive conduct" illustrate this quandary. In the 1992 case of *R.A.V. v. St. Paul*, the Court struck down a Minnesota statute that banned the display of symbols intending to arouse anger "on the basis of race, color, creed, religion, or gender." Outlawing such displays, the Court argued, censored unpopular political messages and violated the First Amendment.

Minnesota's statute was similar to a Virginia law that criminalized behavior that was intentionally threatening or intimidating. This particular law came to national attention in 1998, when a regional Ku Klux Klan leader, Barry Elton Black, was convicted for burning a cross that was visible from a Virginia highway. In another Virginia case that year, two youths were convicted for attempting to burn a cross on the lawn of an interracial couple. Three years later, these cases were consolidated and appealed to the Virginia Supreme Court as *Virginia v. Black*. The state court struck down the lower court's convictions, arguing that such bans on cross burning interfered with freedom of expression.

Virginia v. Black was eventually appealed to the U.S. Supreme Court. In a six-to-three decision in April 2003, the justices declared that states can make it a felony to burn a cross "on the property of another, a highway or other public place . . . with the intent of intimidating any person or group." This ruling upheld the conviction against the Virginia youths who burned a cross on their neighbors' lawn because, in the Court's opinion, such an act "represents an instrument of racial terror so threatening that it overshadows free-speech rights." However, the ruling also upheld the right for the Ku Klux Klan and other groups to burn crosses as a political statement at a rally or a demonstration, even if the cross burning is visible to others. Therefore, since Barry Elton Black had been participating in a constitutionally protected form of speech, his conviction was thrown out.

Writing for the majority, Justice Sandra Day O'Connor granted that the right to free expression has its limits: "The act of burning a cross may mean that a person is engaging in constitutionally proscribable intimidation, or it may mean only that the person is engaged in core political speech." She went on to explain that while a cross burning at a rally might "arouse a sense of anger . . . among the vast majority of citizens," such anger "is not sufficient to ban all cross burnings." Ultimately, however, it remains up to individual states to decide what actions constitute a form of threat or intimidation.

As *Virginia v. Black* reveals, the question of how far the law should go in restricting hate speech—and in supporting the hate groups' rights to express their opinion—remains controversial. The authors in the following chapter explore this topic in more detail as they debate the issues of hate crimes legislation and hate speech on the Internet.

"Hate-crimes legislation is important because it is a message from society . . . that bias crimes will not be tolerated."

Hate-Crime Laws Should Be Supported

Howard P. Berkowitz

Concerned citizens should support laws that increase the penalties for crimes motivated by bigotry, maintains Howard P. Berkowitz in the following viewpoint. Hate crimes are especially devastating because they can inflame community tensions and damage the fabric of a multicultural society. Hate-crime laws are society's way of declaring that bias crimes will not be tolerated, the author points out. Moreover, Berkowitz contends, such laws do not punish people for their beliefs—as critics often claim—but for their criminal actions. Berkowitz is the national chair of the Anti-Defamation League, a non-profit organization that fights racial and ethnic prejudice.

As you read, consider the following questions:
1. Who was Benjamin Nathaniel Smith, according to the author?
2. According to Berkowitz, how many hate crimes were reported in the United States in 1997?
3. What U.S. Supreme Court decision supports the creation of hate-crimes statutes, according to Berkowitz?

Hate crimes, whether directed against one person or many, are particularly destructive in the way they spread feelings of hurt, anxiety and fear. A hate crime is more than an attack on an individual. It is an assault on an entire community. And for this reason alone it is important to send a message that criminals who commit bias crimes will pay the price.

Critics of hate-crimes legislation have used colorful prose to dismiss the laws as "identity politics" and "theatrical empathy," arguing the statutes are a strong-handed attempt to impose a politically correct ideology and an affront to basic constitutional rights.

Shocking Crimes

In recent [times] however, there has been no shortage of horrifying assaults on blacks, Jews and other minorities, which would seem to call this oversimplified view into question. Crimes predicated on race and ethnicity are becoming more and more virulent in this country. They are being committed by individuals with links to organized hate groups operating on the farthest fringes of American society—groups whose outreach is widening due to advances in technology, most notably the Internet.

The crimes have been shocking in their brutality. A man who, according to police, was bent on issuing a "wake-up call to America to kill Jews" builds up an arsenal capable of wreaking vast amounts of bloodshed and barges—guns blazing—into a Jewish community center [in August 1999]. Before his bloody rampage . . . was over, Buford O. Furrow Jr. had shot and wounded 5- and 6-year-olds, a teen-ager and a woman before taking the life of a Filipino-American postal worker whom Furrow identified as a "target of opportunity" because of his race.

Weeks earlier, Benjamin Nathaniel Smith, an avowed racist with ties to the virulently anti-Semitic and racist World Church of the Creator, had gone on a killing rampage through the Midwest. The targets again were minorities—Orthodox Jews on their way home from synagogue, blacks and Asian-Americans. The carnage resulted in the deaths of former basketball coach Ricky Byrdsong and a Korean-American graduate student, slain as he emerged from church in Bloomington, Ind.

Smith's targets also were chosen carefully and, like the three synagogues in Sacramento, Calif., which were damaged by arson in July [1999], his crimes affected people engaged in, or on their way to, worship. Near one of the synagogues in Sacramento, police found hate literature and later discovered evidence possibly linking two brothers arrested in connection with another hate crime—the brutal slaying of a homosexual couple—to the synagogue fires.

Something Must Be Done

All of this recent hate activity has left us, as Americans, grappling for answers. Everyone agrees that something, legislative or otherwise, must be done to stem the tide of hate. The Anti-Defamation League, or ADL, as a leader in the fight against anti-Semitism, hatred and bigotry, believes strong hate-crimes legislation is one answer. We do not view penalty enhancement as a panacea, a cure-all for the scourge of hate in society. But it is important—a rational, fair-minded message to bigots and racists everywhere—that society will not tolerate crimes that single out an individual because of his or her race, religion, national origin or color. Penalty-enhancement statutes put criminals on notice that the consequences for committing hate crimes are severe.

Aside from sensational crimes, government statistics also make a compelling argument for the necessity of strong hate-crimes statutes. Since 1991 the FBI has documented more than 50,000 hate crimes. In 1996 alone, 8,759 hate crimes were reported in the United States. In 1997 . . . the number rose to 9,861—the highest number of hate crimes ever recorded by the FBI in a single year. Still many more hate crimes go undocumented. The numbers continue to rise as the casualties mount.

Legislators across the country, state and federal, recognize the special trauma hate crimes cause, the sense of vulnerability and fear they foster and the polarizing effect they can have on entire communities. Lawmakers understand their responsibility to provide criminal sanctions that reflect our collective societal judgment regarding the relative seriousness of criminal offenses.

While all crimes are upsetting, a hate crime is particularly disturbing because of the unique impact not only on the victim but also on the victim's community. Bias crimes are designed to intimidate, leaving people feeling isolated, vulnerable and unprotected. Failure to address this unique type of crime can cause an isolated incident to explode into widespread community tension. The damage cannot be measured solely in terms of physical injury or dollars and cents. By making minority communities fearful, angry and suspicious of other groups—and of the legal structure that is supposed to protect them—these incidents can damage the fabric of our society and fragment communities.

Opponents' Flawed Arguments

Opponents of hate-crimes legislation often will argue that the laws represent the worst aspects of Orwellian thought control and intrude on the sanctity of the First Amendment. These critics erroneously contend that such statutes punish individuals for their beliefs and their speech. In making this flawed argument, the critics demonstrate a fundamental misunderstanding of hate-crimes legislation as well as the First Amendment.

Not Like Other Crimes

In 1998 . . . over 7,700 hate crimes incidents were reported in our nation, almost one an hour. And it is suspected by the experts that many more go unreported. These are not like other crimes, because these crimes target people simply because of who they are. And because they do, they strike at the heart of who we are as a nation.

Bill Clinton, remarks on proposed hate-crimes legislation, April 25, 2000.

The fact is hate-crimes legislation does not in any way target or punish speech; such statutes punish conduct only. Individuals remain free to express any view about race, religion, sexuality or any other topic. It is only when they act on their prejudices or callously select their victims based on personal characteristics such as race or religion that hate-crimes statutes come into play. Such legislation simply says that someone who attacks a black or a Jew because he is black or Jewish will receive an enhanced penalty. Such an approach by no means is new to criminal law. Legislators, law-enforcement officials and judicial officers frequently consider motive—in charges ranging from the mundane, such as burglary, to the exceptional, such as treason—to determine whether a crime, or what class of crime, has been committed.

The U.S. Supreme Court has supported that view. In 1993, in a landmark 9-0 decision, the court upheld a Wisconsin penalty-enhancement statute, ruling that the state was right in seeking to increase the sentence for an African-American man who had encouraged and participated in an attack on a young white man. In *Wisconsin vs. Mitchell*, the high court ruled that the statute aimed to discourage conduct that is not protected by the First Amendment and that the state had a special interest in punishing bias crimes. The court's decision removed any doubt that legislatures property may increase the penalties for criminal activity in which the victim is targeted because of his race, religion, sexual orientation, gender, ethnicity or disability.

A Message from Society

Hate-crimes legislation is important because it is a message from society and the legislature that bias crimes will not be tolerated. To date, 40 states and the District of Columbia have enacted hate-crimes statutes, as has the federal government. The most effective kind of hate-crimes law, often based on model legislation introduced by the ADL, provides for enhanced penalties when a perpetrator chooses his victim based on race, religion or another protected category. When prejudice prompts an individual to engage in criminal conduct, a prosecutor may seek a more severe sentence but must prove, beyond a reasonable doubt, that the victim intentionally was selected because of personal characteristics. The intent of penalty-enhancement hate-crimes laws is not only to reassure targeted groups by imposing serious punishment of hate-crime perpetrators but also to deter these crimes by demonstrating that they will be dealt with seriously and swiftly.

Constitutional and effective penalty-enhancement statutes must continue to be enacted at the federal and state levels. According to the current federal law—18 U.S.C. Sec. 245

—before the federal government can prosecute a hate crime, it must prove both that the crime occurred because of a person's membership in a designated group and because (not simply while) the victim was engaged in certain specified federally protected activities, such as serving on a jury, voting or attending public schools. Thus, while federal law protects Americans from hate crimes in voting booths and schools, it does not protect them from similar crimes in their homes or on the streets. Presently, it is left to the discretion of the local officials whether to prosecute the crime as a hate crime.

The Hate Crimes Prevention Act . . . would make it easier for the federal government to combat hatred. The act would expand the list of protected categories—currently only race, color, religion and national origin—to include real or perceived sexual orientation, gender and disability. Clearly, then, this would empower the federal government to more effectively protect Americans from bias crimes and to step in when local law-enforcement agencies either cannot or will not act to stop hate.[1]

In these increasingly violent times, hate-crimes legislation is a strong and necessary response to combat criminal acts of prejudice and bias. Current hate-crimes laws are both valuable and constitutional. They only punish acts of violence; they neither condemn private beliefs nor chill constitutionally protected speech. The statutes guarantee that perpetrators of bias crimes will be punished in proportion to the seriousness of the crimes they have committed. The laws protect all Americans, allowing them to walk the streets safe in the knowledge that their community will not tolerate violent bigotry.

---

1. As this volume goes to press, the Hate Crimes Prevention Act has not been signed into law.

"Politically correct hate-crime add-ons are just such a bad idea."

Hate-Crime Laws Are Unnecessary

Jackson Toby

Creating statutes that increase the penalty for bias-motivated crimes is bad policy, argues Jackson Toby in the following viewpoint. Such laws actually force judges to abandon their own discretion and impose an inflexible, mandatory penalty on hate-crime offenders, Toby maintains. These penalties may cause overcrowding in prisons—and early release of serious criminals to make room for hate-crime offenders. Furthermore, since judges are unlikely to give lenient sentences for crimes that upset the public, hate-crime laws are simply unnecessary, the author concludes. Toby is a sociology professor at Rutgers University in New Brunswick, New Jersey.

As you read, consider the following questions:

1. According to Toby, why do most criminal statutes include a range of penalties?
2. What suggests that Michael Melchione may have been wrongly accused of a hate crime, in Toby's view?
3. In the author's opinion, why did Judge Rushton Ridgway initially sentence Charles C. Apprendi to a twelve-year prison term?

Jackson Toby, "Hate-Crime Laws: What's Not to Like?" *Weekly Standard*, vol. 6, October 30, 2000, pp. 24–25. Copyright © 2000 by News Corporation, Weekly Standard. Reproduced by permission.

D uring the second debate between Al Gore and George W. Bush [in the presidential race of 2000], Gore criticized Bush for failing to support a bill that would have toughened the Texas hate-crime law. That measure—named after James Byrd Jr., a black man dragged to his death in Jasper, Texas—failed to pass.[1] Bush defended the way Texas had handled the Byrd case.

> The three men who murdered James Byrd. Guess what's going to happen to them? They're going to be put to death. A jury found them guilty, and it's going to be hard to punish them any worse after they get put to death.

True, a toughened hate-crime law could not have added anything to the penalty in this case. But there are lesser crimes like assault or vandalism where hate-crime statutes can indeed add to the penalty. Moreover, additional categories of people can be protected. For example, the Byrd bill, . . . defined a hate crime as one motivated by the victim's race, ethnicity, sex, disability, religion, or sexual orientation. And the Hate Crimes Prevention Act co-sponsored by Democratic Senator Edward Kennedy of Massachusetts and Republican Senator Gordon H. Smith of Oregon, which the U.S. Senate passed in July [2000], would extend the scope of federal hate-crime protection beyond race, religion, and national origin to gender, sexual orientation, and disability.[2]

Democrats are more enthusiastic than Republicans about expanding the scope of hate-crime laws. President [Bill] Clinton urged the House to follow the lead of the Senate. He said that making attacks on gays a federal hate crime was one of his legislative priorities. Hillary Rodham Clinton, in her race for a Senate seat in New York, told civil rights advocates on the New York City Hall steps on August 23, [2000], that the House of Representatives ought to pass legislation strengthening current laws against hate crimes. She accused her opponent, Rep. Rick Lazio, of not supporting the enhanced federal bill forcefully enough, which his campaign headquarters denied that same day.

Few politicians of either party are willing to declare that

---

1. The bill was reintroduced and signed into law in 2001.   2. As this volume goes to press, this bill had not been signed into law.

hate-crime statutes are simply bad policy. To say that sounds prejudiced. So 42 states and the federal government have now enacted hate-crime laws. Nevada, for example, adds 25 percent to a prison sentence for felonies judged to be hate crimes.

Toughening the penalty when anti-Semitism or hatred of blacks motivates an assault or a murder makes legislators feel virtuous. But such laws do not make sense as public policy for two reasons.

To begin with, they are unnecessary. As Bush pointed out in the debate, in the cases that arouse the most public indignation, conviction already results in very severe penalties: death or life imprisonment. But even with less serious felonies, like armed robbery, existing sentencing procedures already allow room for tougher sentences for more heinous crimes. Second, hate-crime add-ons increase the inefficiency of the criminal justice system by wasting scarce custodial space.

Tying Judges' Hands

Why the laws are unnecessary is fairly obvious. Criminal statutes are written with ranges of penalties, not ordinarily requiring a fixed term of imprisonment. The purpose of doing this is to give judges the opportunity to individualize punishments to fit both the crime and the criminal. Thus judges use their discretion to punish a professional armed robber more severely than the little old lady who gets the dumb idea of supplementing her pension by holding up a neighborhood bank. The judge does not discharge this difficult responsibility alone. He has a probation staff that investigates the offender's background and submits a presentence report on the results of the investigation. When a legislature enacts a hate-crime punishment, on the other hand, it creates a one-size-fits-all penalty that ties the judge's hands once the jury comes in with a guilty verdict.

The second reason hate-crime laws are bad public policy is less obvious. A mandatory sentence for hate-crime offenders forces judges to incarcerate a particular category of criminal for a set period, which may well be longer than he thinks the offender deserves; this is inflexible and possibly unfair. Hate-crime laws leave less room in jails and prisons for others guilty of equally serious or worse misbehavior. A judge who has presided over hundreds of criminal trials for a variety of crimes is in the best position to decide how long an offender should be incarcerated in limited prison space. In many states, overcrowding has forced prison systems to release prisoners whom most citizens consider a public menace.

Clay. © 2001 by Clay Butler. Reprinted by permission.

Two New Jersey cases that applied that state's Ethnic Intimidation Act illustrate both of these failings of hate-crime laws.

Case 1. Thirty-five-year-old Michael Melchione was sentenced on July 14, 2000, in Elizabeth to four years in prison, with no chance of parole until he serves two years, for throwing large rocks at several businesses in Elizabeth owned by Jews or having a Jewish clientele; he had also assaulted a Jewish woman. The Ethnic Intimidation Act overrode the discretion of the judge to take into account, in deciding on the appropriate punishment for Melchione's offense, the degree of viciousness he evinced, his previous criminal record, his employment and family history, and his illness (he is schizophrenic). Owing to his schizophrenia, Melchione may have been guilty of equal-opportunity misbehavior rather than targeting Jews in particular. Alan Silver, an assistant Union County prosecutor, said that without the element of religious bias, Melchione would have faced 180 days in a county jail or possibly probation.

Supreme Court Concerns

Case 2. On June 26, [2000], the U.S. Supreme Court, concerned about fairness, struck down part of New Jersey's hate-crime law in another case. Charles C. Apprendi Jr., a former pharmacist in Vineland, had gotten drunk and shot at the home of a black family in 1994. The Harrell family had just moved into a previously all-white neighborhood. No one was injured, but Apprendi received a 12-year prison term for his crime; the maximum possible sentence would have been 10 years had the judge not considered it a hate crime.

Apprendi had served five and a half years of his sentence when the Supreme Court decided that the Ethnic Intimidation Act should have allowed a *jury* to decide whether Apprendi had indeed committed a hate crime. Note that even after the Supreme Court decision, Judge Rushton H. Ridgway of State Superior Court could have imposed a 10-year sentence, the top of the range of penalties for possessing a weapon for an unlawful purpose. Yet Ridgway apparently had second thoughts about the severity of the penalty he had imposed in 1995. Instead of resentencing Apprendi to ten years, which would have been legal, he resentenced Apprendi, now 45, to seven years and urged the state parole board to take up Apprendi's case as soon as possible. The Cumberland County prosecutor is also supporting a request by Apprendi's lawyer that the board reduce Apprendi's sentence to time served.

Judge Ridgway did not explain why he was more punitive in 1995 than he was [in 2000]. The likelihood is, however, that he was responding to public and media indignation and to the pain of the victimized family. Crime victims are encouraged to express to the court their views on the appropriate sentence. The black family whose house was fired on understandably favored the severest sentence possible. Six years later the Harrell family still feels that a lesser sentence for Apprendi now would be "a slap on the wrist" given the pain he caused.

Unnecessary "Add-Ons"

In the Melchione case, too, victims and victim-defense organizations pressured the court for harsh sentences. Charles Goldstein, regional director of the Anti-Defamation League of B'nai B'rith, was pleased by the four-year sentence given to Melchione. "This decision demonstrates unequivocally that those who commit bias crimes will go to jail," he commented outside the courtroom.

In short, even without special hate-crime legislation judges are unlikely to give lenient sentences within the range provided for the offense for any crime that upsets the public, as hate crimes do. When Victor Hugo said that an army could be resisted but not an idea whose time has come, he was thinking of a *good* idea. But the time can come for a *bad* idea too. Politically correct hate-crime add-ons are just such a bad idea. They are unnecessary and have served mainly to make the criminal justice system more unwieldy and less fair.

> "It may be worth considering some very limited restrictions on some hate expression."

Internet Hate Speech Should Be Restricted

Laura Leets

In the following viewpoint Laura Leets argues that some restrictions on Internet hate speech are warranted. Leets has conducted research suggesting that the effects of racist propaganda are not immediately obvious. Hate speech can foster the development of bigoted beliefs that may emerge gradually or remain dormant until the social climate becomes conducive to hate crimes, she contends. Since the Internet is such a wide-reaching forum for disseminating information, legislators should consider ways to restrict hate expression and racist indoctrination in cyberspace. Leets is an an assistant professor in the communications department at Stanford University.

As you read, consider the following questions:

1. How did Leets conduct her study on the effects of hate speech?
2. According to Susan Opotow, what is moral exclusion?
3. What is the difference between deterministic and probabilistic effects, according to Leets?

Laura Leets, "Should All Speech Be Free?" *The Quill*, vol. 89, May 2001, p. 38. Copyright © 2001 by Society of Professional Journalists. Reproduced by permission of the author.

There's been a groundswell in the past several years to increase diversity in journalism, both in news coverage and in newsroom staffing. The goal of several diversity initiatives is to increase the number of voices that regularly appear in our newspapers, magazines, broadcasts and Web sites.

It's important to seek different perspectives and ideas, and the goal of such initiatives is an admirable and productive one. There are some voices, however, that have demonstrably adverse effects. So while the journalism community, judicial system and American public generally support tolerance of diverse viewpoints, some perspectives and types of speech still warrant concern.

One problematic voice is that of hate. Whether it is the dragging death of an African-American behind a pick-up truck in Texas, a gay student's murder in Wyoming, a racially motivated shooting spree at a Los Angeles Jewish community center or a bloody rampage by two high school students enamored of Hitler's fascism, the rising incidence of hate crimes and the groups who appear to encourage them is attracting public interest. In particular, the World Wide Web has provided marginalized extremist groups a more notable and accessible public platform. The Internet has put the problem of incendiary hate into sharp relief.

Long-Term Effects of Hate Speech

In several research studies where I have focused on short-term message effects of hate speech, it is difficult to demonstrate with certainty the linkage between hate expression and violence or harm (deterministic causality). In a recent study, I asked 266 participants (both university and non-university students recruited online) to read and evaluate one of 11 white supremacist Web pages that I had randomly sampled from the Internet. Similar to previous studies, the data showed that the content of the hate Web pages was perceived to be in keeping with the Court bounds for First Amendment protection. Yet the participants acknowledged an indirect effect that, on the other hand, may suggest hate speech effects are more slow-acting—and thus imperceptible in the short term (probabilistic causality).

Specifically, participants in the cyberhate study rated the

indirect threats from the World Church of the Creator (WCOTC) Web page as very high (Mean=6, on a seven-point scale where seven represented the highest score). Is it coincidental that a former WCOTC member recently shot 11 Asian Americans, African-Americans and Jews, killing two, before committing suicide? Or that two brothers associated with WCOTC were charged with murdering a gay couple and fire-bombing three Sacramento synagogues? While WCOTC leader Matthew Hale does not endorse this lawlessness, neither does he condemn it. Part of their ideology is that all nonwhites are "mud people," people without souls, like animals eligible for harm.

Blurring Fantasy and Reality

The combination of intimacy and distance in cyberspace provides a new context for racist harassment. Racists began by sending "mail bombs" or a truck-load of junk mail to crash their victims' computer systems. More recently they started using digital tools to offer the "pleasure" of simulated racial violence. For example, a photograph of a young black man, face down on the floor being beaten and kicked, used to be posted on the Skinheads USA website until a police investigation [stopped it]. By blurring the line between reality and fantasy, this kind of violence is politically slippery but very dangerous.

Cyberculture has also given a new lease on life to the "International Jew" as an omnipresent figure of hate. The Internet's global framework enhances a historical component of antiSemitism: the notion of an international conspiracy. The "traditional" products of the racist imagination are now circulating further than ever before.

Les Back, *UNESCO Courier*, January 2001.

Current legal remedies may be missing the real harm of racist indoctrination, which may not be immediately apparent or verifiable. For instance, hate expressions tend to encourage a set of beliefs that develop gradually and that often can lie dormant until conditions are ripe for a climate of moral exclusion and subsequent crimes against humanity. Moral exclusion is defined by Susan Opotow, an independent scholar affiliated with Teachers College at Columbia University, as the psychosocial orientation toward individuals or groups for whom justice principles or considerations of fairness are not applicable. People who are morally excluded are perceived as nonentities, and harming them appears acceptable and just (e.g., slavery, holocaust).

It is not the abstract viewpoints that are problematic. Rather, it is the expressions intending to elicit persecution or oppression that often begin with dehumanizing rhetoric. In my research, I argue that communication is the primary means by which psychological distancing occurs. Arguably, it may be the long-term, not short-term, effects of hate expression that are potentially more far reaching.

The Question of Internet Regulation

Even though prevailing First Amendment dogma maintains that speech may not be penalized merely because its content is racist, sexist or basically abhorrent, Internet law is a dynamic area and as such is not completely integrated into our regulatory and legal system. Consequently, many questions remain about how traditional laws should apply to this new and unique medium.

The Internet can combine elements of print (newspapers and magazines), broadcast (television and radio) and face-to-face interaction. Moreover, unlike users of previous media, those on the Internet have the power to reach a mass audience, but in this case the audience must be more active in seeking information, as cyberspace is less intrusive than other mass media.

It is unclear whether content-based restrictions found in other technological media may be permissible for the Internet. For example, the FCC ruled that indecency was unsuitable for broadcast media because of ease of access, invasiveness and spectrum scarcity, yet cable and print media are not subjected to this form of content regulation.

In 1996, the United States Congress passed the Telecommunications Bill, which included the Communications Decency Act (CDA). The CDA regulated indecent or obscene material for adults on the Internet, applying First Amendment jurisprudence from broadcast and obscenity cases. Later that year, the Supreme Court declared two provisions unconstitutional in *Reno vs. ACLU*. Congress and the Court disagreed on the medium-specific constitutional speech standard suitable for the World Wide Web. Congress argued that the Internet should be regulated in the same manner as television or radio, but the Court decided not to apply that doctrinal framework. Instead, the Court viewed the Internet as face-to-face communication, deserving full protection.

Issues of Internet regulation naturally lead to the question of whether such regulation is even possible. Cyberspace doesn't have geographical boundaries, so it is difficult to determine where violations of the law should be prosecuted. There are enforcement conflicts, not only between different countries' legal jurisdictions, but also among federal, state and local levels in the United States. Although Americans place a high premium on free expression, without much effort most people can find Internet material that they would want to censor.

Determining Cause and Effect

Some argue that cyberhate oversteps this idea of "mere insult" and warrants liability. The Internet is a powerful forum of communication with its broad (world-wide) reach, interactivity and multi-media capability to disseminate information. These features inevitably result in concerns about impact, especially when viewed as empowering racists and other extremists. It is common for people to wonder whether white supremacist Web pages cause hate crime. This question is similar to people's concerns regarding whether TV violence causes aggression in viewers. The issue of causation (claim: x causes y) is an important one to address.

It is important to differentiate between language determining (or causing) an effect and language influencing the probability of an effect. In terms of a strict social science approach (deterministic causation) we can't say language has an effect unless three conditions are met: (a) there must be a relationship between the hypothesized cause and the observed effect, (b) the cause must always precede the effect in time (x must come before y), and (c) all alternative explanations for the effect must be eliminated. The problem with making a strong case for a causal effect lies with the second and third conditions. For example, most media (television, Internet etc.) effects are probabilistic, not deterministic. It is almost impossible to make a clear case for television or cyberhate effects because the relationship is almost never a simple causal one. Instead, there are many factors in the influence process. Each factor increases the probability of an effect occurring. The effects process is complex.

The U.S. Supreme Court has traditionally viewed speech effects in terms of short-term, deterministic consequences, and has not considered more far-reaching effects.

While more research is needed on the long-term effects of hate speech, it may be worth considering some very limited restrictions on some hate expression. American jurisprudence has not fully realized the harmful nature and effects stemming from hate speech, which has the ability both to directly elicit immediate behavior (short term) and to cultivate an oppressive climate (long term).

"One man's hate speech is another man's political statement."

Internet Hate Speech Should Not Be Restricted

Charles Levendosky

According to Charles Levendosky in the following viewpoint, restricting Internet hate speech would undermine democracy. To begin with, he argues, no government or organization can accurately define hate speech because what one person may find offensive may be considered a legitimate political statement by another. In fact, he asserts, restricting hate speech could result in the suppression of unpopular political movements, which are vital to the health of democracies. Moreover, allowing the powerless to vent their frustrations harmlessly through controversial speech actually prevents violence, Levendosky claims. He also contends that granting the government control over offensive speech will invite it to control all media. Levendosky is the editorial page editor and a syndicated columnist for the *Casper Star-Tribune* in Wyoming.

As you read, consider the following questions:
1. How does Levendosky define hate speech?
2. According to the author, what historic political movements used inflammatory rhetoric to effect change?
3. What happened when the Supreme Court of Canada adopted feminists Catharine MacKinnon and Andrea Dworkin's thesis that pornography harms women, according to Levendosky?

Another free speech battle has begun to shape up. This one isn't about sex; it's about hate speech. It pits those who want to prohibit hatemongering on the Internet against those who believe that the First Amendment must protect even that speech—no matter how despicable.

Hate speech on the Internet has grown rapidly—through websites, email, bulletin boards and chat rooms—according to a study published by the Anti-Defamation League last year. The ADL monitors the Internet looking for anti-Semitic speech propagated by neo-Nazi, white supremacist groups. In the study, "High-Tech Hate: Extremist Use of the Internet," the ADL notes that hate websites more than doubled in one year, from 1996 to 1997. The organization estimates their number to be 250. And pressure is mounting to shut down these sites, or at least, to limit access to them.

Curtailing Hate Speech

According to a *Washington Post* story dated October 24, 1997, the ADL is working with America Online to develop software to filter out hate sites.

In 1997, the United Nations held a seminar in Geneva to discuss how to curtail hate speech on the Internet.

In April 1998, the Australia B'nai B'rith Anti-Defamation Commission petitioned Australia's Internet Industry Association to make racist websites illegal in that nation.

And on August 2, 1998, the *New York Times* reported that Canada, using that country's anti-hate legislation, has begun cracking down on hate speech on the Internet.

Hate speech can be loosely defined as speech that reviles or ridicules a person or group of people based upon their race, creed, sexual orientation, religion, handicap, economic condition or national origin.

HateWatch also monitors hate-group activities on the Internet. David Goldman, director of HateWatch, estimates that more than 200 active racist, anti-Semitic, anti-gay, Holocaust denial, Christian Identity, black racist, anti-Arab, anti-Christian pages can currently be found on the Internet.

Goldman credits Don Black, the ex-Grand Dragon of the Knights of the Ku Klux Klan's Realm of Alabama with creating the first racist website, Stormfront, in March

1995. Stormfront is still online.

HateWatch has taken a different approach to hate websites. The organization is in the process of "adopting" domain names (URLs) which might otherwise be used by hate groups. They are asking donations to acquire such domain names as "aryan-nations.org," "whitepower.net," and "kukluxklan.net." It's a creative strategy, but one which seems doomed to failure.

The range of possible domain names connected to any hate group is only limited by the imagination. If the domain name "whitepower.net" if already registered, one could shift to "snowpower.net," or use "pure-nations.org" for the aryan domain.

At present, the World Wide Web contains skinhead and while supremacist sites with names like Hammerskin Nation, Delaware Skingirl Crew, Orgullo Skinheads, Bootgirl88, Skinhead Pride, SS Bootboys, White Aryan Resistance, White World of Skinchick, Siegheil88, Hatemongers' Hangout, Skinz, Northern HammerSkins. The list tops 130—of just these groups.

There are anti-gay websites with names like The American Guardian, Cyber Nationalist Group (CNG), God Hates Fags, RevWhites Christian Politics, and Society To Remove All Immoral Godless Homosexual Trash (STRAIGHT).

The Internet parade of hate includes the anti-Muslim websites (The Glistrup Homepage and Faelleslisten), the anti-Arab sites (Jewish Defense League and the Kahane Homepage), the anti-Christian sites (Altar of Unholy Blasphemy and Chorazaim), anti-Semitic sites (Radio Islam and Jew Watch), black racist sites (House of David, and The Blackmind), Holocaust denial sites (Adelaide Institute and Annwn Publications), neo-Nazi sites (Alpha and Fourth Reich), and Christian Identity sites (America's Promise Ministries and IaHUeH's Kingdom).

A number of universities in the United States, more sensitive to people's feelings than the significance of the First Amendment, have written speech regulations to punish students who post hate messages on the World Wide Web. Some universities have put blocking technology on their computers that have Internet access—to filter out websites that advocate racism, anti-Semitism, white supremacy, homophobia, Holocaust denial, sexual superiority, anti-government vigilante justice, and other forms of prejudice and bigotry.

There are those organizations, like the ADL, that push for a rating system for every web page, with stiff fines for those who don't rate their sites or rate them wrongly. Presumably an Aryan Nations or Ku Klux Klan site would have to rate itself (or be rated by others) so that children could not gain access when the appropriate filtering program is installed to read the ratings and block some categories.

The Southern Poverty Law Center in Montgomery, Alabama, recently labelled the Nation of Islam as a hate group in an intelligence report, because of anti-Semitic comments made by Minister Louis Farrakhan.

Interestingly enough, neither the ADL nor HateWatch nor even the Southern Poverty Law Center lists the Jewish Defense Organization as a group that spews hate on its website.

Who makes the decision about which websites cross the line into hate speech? The federal government? Internet service providers?

A few months ago, Microsystems Software, the manufacturer that makes the filter called Cyber Patrol, decided to block out the American Family Association's website because it contains prejudicial statements against homosexuals. The rightwing American Family Association, ironically, has pushed parents, schools and libraries to use Internet filters, including Cyber Patrol.

Richard Delgado, Jean Stefancic and other academics argue in *Must We Defend Nazis? Hate Speech, Pornography, and the New First Amendment* that hate speech should not be protected by the First Amendment. Fortunately, their arguments have not been persuasive against our long and honored tradition of free speech.

While we may despise the comments made on some of these hate-filled websites, it is difficult to argue they are not espousing political positions. Often one man's hate speech is another man's political statement. And political commentary has—and should continue to have—the highest First Amendment protection.

White supremacist David Duke, who was recently elected

to lead the Republican Party in the largest GOP parish in the state of Louisiana, has a website that denigrates blacks. His political stature is built on his racism. Certainly, his web page, hate and all, is a political statement.

Duke explains why the KKK and other white power groups have flocked to the Internet: "As the new millennium approaches, one can feel the currents of history moving swiftly around us. The same race that created the brilliant technology of the Internet, will—through this powerful tool—be awakened from its long sleep." And, indeed, white supremacist websites are some of the most technologically sophisticated on the Internet.

As the U.S. Supreme Court noted in finding the Communications Decency Act unconstitutional last year, anyone with access to the Internet can be a pamphleteer sending email messages to thousands of recipients with one click of a button, or posting websites that are eventually seen by hundreds of thousands. It is the most democratic communication media yet devised. However, to remain truly democratic, it must allow any viewpoint to be posted and debated.

Crushing Socio-Political Movements

The leading edge of any social or political movement cuts a path to recognition by using radical, sometimes outrageous rhetoric. The rhetoric is there to define or redefine the landscape in terms that suit that particular movement. It is there to shake up the prevailing state of affairs. This has been true in this nation from the time of our own revolution to gain independence from Great Britain to the present. Certainly, the British Crown could have considered the Declaration of Independence a form of hate speech.

The Industrial Workers of the World, the labor movement, the socialist movement, anti-war movements, the Black Power movement, poverty marches, veteran's marches, the temperance crusade, the women's liberation movement, the anti-abortion movement—all used inflammatory rhetoric like a blowtorch to burn a hole in the status quo. To demand that people take sides. And see the world differently.

If hate speech were prohibited, socio-political movements could be crushed before they even started.

Hate Speech Is Protected

How do you stop a bully from terrorizing the playground? Get him to pick a fight with an even bigger bully. With the rise of Internet hate, virtual bigots have effectively picked a fight with government and constitutional authorities, prompting some officials to suggest that free speech laws be overturned in order to eliminate hateful speech. Citing the successful removal of the violently anti-abortionist "Nuremberg Files" site from the Internet, censorship advocates argue that outlawing hate speech is the most expedient way to curtail virtual bigotry.

The "Nuremberg Files" were banned, however, not because of inherently hateful speech but because a court determined that they presented a genuine threat of physical harm to doctors and nurses who perform abortions. Hate sites in the United States remain protected by the First Amendment unless they can be clearly linked to concrete threats or acts.

Stacia Brown, *Sojourners*, September/October 2000.

The current cliche about "civility" in debate may be fine when we all agree to basic premises and we're all well-fed and treated equally. We can afford to be polite to one another and even friendly. But civility does not serve the downtrodden, the forgotten, the invisible, the persecuted, the hungry and homeless. Civility in pursuit of justice plays to the power structure's selective deafness. To be effective, the voice must be raised, the tone sharpened, the language at a pitch that slices the air. Americans know this at heart—we were born in a revolution.

The Danger of Suppressing Speech

Hate speech is not the cause of bigotry, but arises out of it and a sense of political and social powerlessness. Allowing those who see themselves as powerless to speak—no matter how vehement the language—salves the speaker. Venting frustration, anger, and hurt is an important use of language. It may actually short circuit an inclination for physical violence.

The black playwright Imamu Amiri Baraka (LeRoi Jones) illustrated this principle in *Dutchman*, a 1960s play about a black rebellion. One of his characters yells at a white woman riding on the same train, "And I'm the great would-be poet. Yes. That's right! Poet. Some kind of bastard literature . . .

all it needs is a simple knife thrust. Just let me bleed you, you loud whore, and one poem vanished. . . . If Bessie Smith had killed some white people she wouldn't have needed that music."

Suppressing speech, even hateful speech and perhaps especially hateful speech, would inevitably lead to violence.

We don't protect the civil rights of those who are targets of hateful speech by suppressing the speech of hate mongers. For eventually, inexorably, such suppression turns and bites those it is supposed to protect.

When civil liberties are lost, civil rights follow. When a chunk is carved out of First Amendment protections, we all lose a portion of our rights as citizens.

Speech laws that have been adopted to protect racial minorities are actually used to persecute the very people they were created to protect. This has been true in Great Britain and in Canada—just as it has been true at universities in the United States.

When the Supreme Court of Canada adopted the Catharine MacKinnon/Andrea Dworkin thesis that pornography is harmful to women, the very first groups to be targeted by the Canadian government were gay and lesbian bookstores. Two of Andrea Dworkin's own books (*Woman Hating* and *Pornography: Men Possessing Women*) were seized at the Canadian border by customs officials. The books were adjudged to be "pornography" and thereby harmful to women.

Those who censor others, eventually censor themselves. They bury their own messages.

When the University of Michigan put its speech code against racist speech into effect and before the code was struck down in 1989 as unconstitutional, 20 students were charged with violations. Ironically only one was punished, a black student for using the term "white trash."

It was no accident that the first person to be charged under a U.S. hate crime enhancement law was a black man. It added years to his sentence.

The power structure interprets and enforces the law. Where white males dominate, white males are less likely to be prosecuted under such laws—a cynical observation, but true.

Stifling Dissent and Protest

If the federal government were to be given the authority to limit speech on the Internet, that authority would spread to all media. And the government would have the unholy power to stifle dissent and protest.

Suppressing hate speech is more dangerous than allowing it to exist. Like it or not, hate speech has a role to play in a nation dedicated to vigorous debate about public issues.

If we come to a point in our history when we fear messages that we despise, then we will have lost the strength and will to govern ourselves. Or as the great First Amendment scholar Alexander Meiklejohn put it so succinctly when testifying before Congress in 1955, "To be afraid of any idea is to be unfit for self-government."

Periodical Bibliography

The following articles have been selected to supplement the diverse views presented in this chapter.

Richard D. Barton — "A Free Nation Can Overcome the Forces of Hate," *San Diego Union-Tribune*, August 15, 1999.

Elizabeth Birch and Paul Weyrich — "Q: Should Hate-Crime Laws Explicitly Protect 'Sexual Orientation?'" (Symposium), *Insight*, July 24, 2000.

Morris Dees — "Hate Crimes," *Vital Speeches of the Day*, February 1, 2000.

Jonathan Gatehouse — "No Real Excuse: There Are Times When an Apology Is Not Enough," *Maclean's*, December 2002.

Ted Gup — "When Hate Collides with Free Speech," *Washington Post National Weekly Edition*, December 23, 2002.

Bob Herbert — "America's Twin Evils," *New York Times*, August 15, 1999.

Gara Lamarche — "The Price of Hate," *Index on Censorship*, March/April 1999.

Richard John Neuhaus — "Why 'Hate Crimes' Are Wrong," *First Things*, January 1999.

Keith Perine — "The Trouble with Regulating Hate," *Network World*, July 24, 2000.

Katha Pollitt — "Hate Crimes Legislation," *Nation*, November 29, 1999.

Susan Raffo — "Thinking About Hate Crimes," *Z Magazine*, January 1999.

Robert Scheer — "Shine Light on the Dark Side of the Net," *Los Angeles Times*, August 8, 1999.

Eric Tischler — "Can Tolerance Be Taught?" *Corrections Today*, August 1999.

Robert Tracinski — "Politicizing Crime," *Intellectual Activist*, April 1999.

Wall Street Journal — "Hate and Punishment," May 18, 2001.

For Further Discussion

Chapter 1

1. Earl Ofari Hutchinson maintains that the incidence of hate crimes against Muslims and Arabs has increased since the terrorist attacks of September 11, 2001. James Lacey argues that hate-crime statistics are distorted by political influences and that hate crimes against Muslims and those perceived as Middle Eastern are relatively rare. What evidence do these authors present to support their conclusions? Which of these arguments is more persuasive? Why?

2. Ellen Goodman contends that hate crimes threaten communities and therefore deserve punishments beyond those given for ordinary crimes. Nat Hentoff counters that hate-crime convictions elevate politically correct victims over others. Based on your reading of the chapter, do you think acts of violence motivated by hate against a specific group should be considered a hate crime and subject to additional penalties? Why or why not?

3. Based on your readings of the viewpoints in this chapter, do you think hate crimes are a serious problem? Defend your answer using examples from the viewpoints.

Chapter 2

1. Sarah J. McCarthy maintains that the rhetoric of the religious right contributes to a climate of hate and violence in the United States. Mark Tooley disagrees, contending that liberals are wrongly stigmatizing traditional religious beliefs as hateful. Both of these authors' arguments incorporate anecdotal examples and some statements made by individuals with whom they disagree. In your opinion, which author uses these examples and quotes to better effect? Explain your answer.

2. After reading the viewpoints by Stephan Lhotzky, David Tyler, and Leonard Zeskind, compare the growth of hate groups in Germany with the development of today's American hate groups. In what ways are the factors contributing to the increase in German hate groups similar to the factors contributing to American hate groups? How do the German and American situations differ? Defend your answer with examples from the viewpoints.

3. The authors in this chapter present several arguments describing what might motivate people to commit hate crimes or join hate groups. Compare the various viewpoints, then formulate

and explain your own opinion on what provokes people to engage in hate crimes.

Chapter 3

1. Carl Rowan argues that hate groups pose a grave threat because they are becoming more organized. Anthony B. Robinson suggests that hate crimes are often committed by the mentally ill, and that Americans should avoid laying the blame for such crimes on hate groups. Based on your reading of this chapter, how serious of a threat do you believe hate groups present? Defend your answer with examples from the viewpoints.

2. Daniel Levitas believes that the extreme right has neither the funds nor the organizational prowess to affect mainstream politics. However, he also argues that the terrorist attacks of September 11, 2001, have given the far right "plenty of highly charged racial issues . . . to inflame and exploit." In your observation of events during the first decade of the twenty-first century, do you see evidence that supports Levitas' claim? Explain.

3. John M. Cotter maintains that white supremacists use white power music to spread racist propaganda and to incite violence. Eric Owens contends that white power music promotes positive social values and racial pride among white youth. Cotter was a political science Ph.D. student when he wrote his viewpoint while Owens identifies himself as a Celtic folk musician and fan of the skinhead movement. How do the backgrounds of these two authors influence your assessment of their arguments? Explain your answer.

Chapter 4

1. Howard P. Berkowitz argues that hate-crime laws send a message to racists and bigots that violence motivated by their beliefs will not be tolerated. Jackson Toby contends that extra penalties for hate crimes are unnecessary because people who commit such crimes are likely to receive strong sentences in the first place. Which viewpoint do you agree with, and why?

2. Laura Leets maintains that the potentially dangerous long-term effects of hate speech justify limited restrictions on Internet hate sites. How would Charles Levendosky respond to Leets' contention? In your opinion, which author presents better suggestions for challenging hate on the Internet? Explain.

Organizations to Contact

The editors have compiled the following list of organizations concerned with the issues debated in this book. The descriptions are derived from materials provided by the organizations. All have publications or information available for interested readers. The list was compiled on the date of publication of the present volume; the information provided here may change. Be aware that many organizations take several weeks or longer to respond to inquiries, so allow as much time as possible.

American-Arab Anti-Discrimination Committee (ADC)
4201 Connecticut Ave., Washington, DC 20008
(202) 244-2990 • fax: (202) 244-3196
e-mail: adc@adc.org • website: www.adc.org

ADC is a nonsectarian, nonpartisan civil rights organization dedicated to combating discrimination against people of Arab heritage and promoting intercultural awareness. It works to protect Arab American rights through a national network of chapters. The committee publishes the newsletter *ADC Times* ten times a year as well as an annual special report summarizing incidents of hate crimes, discrimination, and defamation against Arab Americans.

American Civil Liberties Union (ACLU)
125 Broad St., 18th Fl., New York, NY 10004
(212) 549-2585
website: www.aclu.org

The ACLU is a national organization that works to defend Americans' civil rights guaranteed in the U.S. Constitution. The ACLU publishes the semiannual newsletter *Civil Liberties Alert* as well as the briefing papers "Hate Speech on Campus" and "Racial Justice."

Anti-Defamation League (ADL)
823 United Nations Plaza, New York, NY 10017
(212) 490-2525
website: www.adl.org

The ADL is an international organization that fights prejudice and extremism. It collects, organizes, and distributes information about anti-Semitism, hate crimes, bigotry, and racism, and also monitors hate groups and extremists on the Internet. Its many publications include the report *Hate on the World Wide Web*, the brochure "Close the Book on Hate: 101 Ways to Combat Prejudice," and the book *Hate Hurts: How Children Learn and Unlearn Prejudice*.

Aryan Nations
Church of Jesus Christ Christian
PO Box 362, Hayden, ID 83835
(208) 772-2408
e-mail: pastorbutler@twelvearyannations.com
website: www.twelvearyannations.com

Believing that whites are God's chosen people, Aryan Nations and the Church of Jesus Christ Christian maintain that nonwhites are soulless beings and that Jews are the offspring of the devil. It publishes the *Aryan Nations Newsletter* and pamphlets such as *New World Order in North America*, *Aryan Warriors Stand*, and *Know Your Enemies*.

Canadian Centre on Racism and Prejudice
Box 505, Station Desjardins, Montreal, Quebec H5B 1B6 Canada
(514) 727-2936

Affiliated with the Center for Democratic Renewal in Atlanta, Georgia, the Canadian center monitors the activities of white supremacist groups and the development of the far right in Canada. It publishes the bimonthly newsletter *Bulletin*.

Center for Democratic Renewal
PO Box 50469, Atlanta, GA 30302
(404) 221-0025 • fax: (404) 221-0045
website: www.publiceye.org/cdr/cdr.html

This nonprofit organization monitors hate group and white supremacist activity in America and opposes bias-motivated violence. It is affiliated with Political Research Associates, a nonprofit research center that studies "antidemocratic, authoritarian, and other oppressive movements, institutions, and trends." The CDR publishes the book *When Hate Groups Come to Town*.

Center for the Study of Hate and Extremism
Department of Criminal Justice
College of Social and Behavioral Sciences
California State University, San Bernardino
5500 University Pkwy., San Bernardino, CA 92407
e-mail: blevin8@aol.com • website: www.hatemonitor.org

The Center for the Study of Hate and Extremism is a nonpartisan research and policy center that investigates the ways that bigotry, extremism, and terrorism deny civil or human rights to people on the basis of race, ethnicity, religion, gender, sexual orientation, disability, or other relevant status characteristics. The center seeks to aid scholars, community activists, government officials, law enforcement, the media, and others with objective information to aid them in their examination and implementation of law and policy.

Euro-American Alliance
PO Box 2-1776, Milwaukee, WI 53221
(414) 423-0565

This organization opposes racial mixing and advocates self-segregation for whites. It publishes a number of pamphlets, including *Who Hates Whom?* and *Who We Really Are*.

Human Rights and Race Relations Centre
120 Eglinton Dr. East, Suite 500, Toronto, Ontario M4P 1E2, Canada
(416) 481-7793

The center is a charitable organization that opposes all types of discrimination. Its goal is to develop a society free of racism, in which each ethnic group respects the rights of other groups. It recognizes individuals and institutions that excel in the promotion of race relations or work for the elimination of discrimination. The center publishes the weekly newspaper *New Canada*.

Human Rights Campaign (HRC)
919 18th St. NW, Washington, DC 20006
(202) 628-4160 • fax: (202) 347-5323
e-mail: hrc@hrc.org • website: www.hrc.org

Founded in 1980, the HRC is the largest gay and lesbian political organization in the United States. The HRC seeks to protect the civil rights of gay, lesbian, bisexual, and transgendered Americans. It lobbies the federal government on gay, lesbian, and AIDS issues, fights discriminatory legislation, and supports the Employment Non-Discrimination Act (ENDA), a bill that would protect Americans from being terminated from their jobs on grounds of sexual orientation. The HRC also sponsors the National Coming Out Project.

National Alliance
PO Box 90, Hillsboro, WV 24946
(304) 653-4600
e-mail: national@natvan.com • website: www.natvan.com

The alliance believes that the white race is superior to all other races in intelligence, ability, and creativity. It argues that it is the obligation of all whites to fight for the creation of a white nation that is free of non-Aryan influence. It publishes the newsletter *Free Speech* and the magazine *National Vanguard*.

National Association for the Advancement of Colored People (NAACP)
4805 Mt. Hope Dr., Baltimore, MD 21215-3297
(410) 358-8900 • fax: (410) 486-9255 • hot line: (410) 521-4939
website: www.naacp.org
The NAACP is the oldest and largest civil rights organization in the United States. Its principal objective is to ensure the political, educational, social, and economic equality of minorities. It publishes the magazine *Crisis* ten times a year as well as a variety of newsletters, books, and pamphlets.

National Coalition Against Censorship
275 Seventh Ave., New York, NY 10001
(212) 807-6222 • fax: (212) 807-6245
e-mail: ncac@ncac.org • website: www.ncac.org
The coalition represents more than forty national organizations that work to prevent suppression of free speech and the press. It publishes the quarterly *Censorship News.*

National Gay and Lesbian Task Force (NGLTF)
1700 Kalorama Rd. NW, Washington, DC 20009-2624
(202) 332-6483 • fax: (202) 332-0207
e-mail: ngltf@ngltf.org • website: www.ngltf.org
NGLTF is a civil rights organization that fights bigotry and violence against gays and lesbians. It sponsors conferences and organizes local groups to promote civil rights legislation for gays and lesbians. It publishes the monthly *Eye on Equality* column and distributes reports, fact sheets, and bibliographies on antigay violence.

People for the American Way Foundation
2000 M St. NW, Suite 400, Washington, DC 20036
e-mail: pfaw@pfaw.org • website: www.pfaw.org
People for the American Way Foundation opposes the political agenda of the religious right. Through public education, lobbying, and legal advocacy, the foundation works to defend equal rights. The foundation publishes *Hostile Climate*, a report detailing intolerant incidents directed against gays and lesbians, and organizes the Students Talk About Race (STAR) program, which trains college students to lead high school discussions on intergroup relations.

Southern Poverty Law Center (SLPC)
400 Washington Ave., Montgomery, AL 36104
(334) 956-8200
websites: www.splcenter.org • www.tolerance.org

The center litigates civil cases to protect the rights of poor people, particularly when those rights are threatened by white supremacist and other hate groups. The affiliated Intelligence Project monitors hate groups and extremist activity throughout the United States and publishes the quarterly *Intelligence Report*. SPLC also sponsors an anti-bias education project, Teaching Tolerance, dedicated to helping teachers foster equity, respect and understanding in the classroom and beyond. In addition to the biannual *Teaching Tolerance* magazine, the monthly *SPLC Report* and the brochures *Responding to Hate at School* and *Ten Ways to Fight Hate* are available through the center.

Stormfront

PO Box 6637, West Palm Beach, FL 33405
(561) 833-0030 • fax: (561) 820-0051
e-mail: comments@stormfront.org • website: www.stormfront.org

Stormfront is dedicated to preserving "white western culture, ideals, and freedom of speech." It serves as a resource for white political and social action groups. It publishes the weekly newsletter Stormwatch, and its website contains articles and position papers such as *White Nationalism: Key Concepts* and *Equality: Man's Most Dangerous Myth*.

White Aryan Resistance (WAR)

PO Box 65, Fallbrook, CA 92088
(760) 723-8996
e-mail: warmetzger@sbcglobal.net • website: www.resist.com

WAR believes the white race is in danger of extinction and advocates for a separatist state for whites only. It publishes the monthly newspaper *WAR*, produces the *War Radio* show, distributes "white power" music recordings, and maintains a racial news and information hot line.

Bibliography of Books

Kathleen Blee — *Inside Organized Racism: Women in the Hate Movement.* Berkeley: University of California Press, 2002.

Howard L. Bushart, John R. Craig, and Myra Barnes — *Soldiers of God: White Supremacists and Their Holy War for America.* New York: Kensington, 1998.

Richard Delgado and Jean Stefancic — *Must We Defend Nazis? Hate Speech, Pornography, and the First Amendment.* New York: New York University Press, 1997.

Betty A. Dobratz and Stephanie L. Shanks-Meile — *"White Power, White Pride!": The White Separatist Movement in the United States.* New York: Twayne, 1997.

David Duke — *My Awakening.* Mandeville, LA: Free Speech Press, 2000.

Valerie Jenness and Ryken Grattet — *Making Hate a Crime: From Social Movement Concept to Law Enforcement Practice.* New York: Russell Sage Foundation, 2001.

Sandra E. Johnson — *Standing on Holy Ground: A Battle Against Hate Crime in the Deep South.* New York: St. Martin's, 2002.

Janis L. Judson and Donna M. Bertazzoni — *Law, Media, and Culture: The Landscape of Hate.* New York: Peter Lang, 2002.

Joyce King — *Hate Crime: The Story of a Dragging in Jasper, Texas.* New York: Knopf, 2002.

Frederick M. Lawrence — *Punishing Hate: Bias Crime Under American Law.* Cambridge, MA: Harvard University Press, 2002.

LegiSchool Project — *Hate Behavior and Hate Crimes: What Motivates People to Hate? How Can We Prevent Hate Crimes in Our Schools and Communities?* Sacramento, CA: Senate Publications, 2000.

Jack Levin and Jack McDevitt — *Hate Crimes Revisited: America's War on Those Who Are Different.* Boulder, CO: Westview Press, 2002.

Daniel Levitas — *The Terrorist Next Door: The Militia Movement and the Radical Right.* Gordonville, VA: Thomas Dunne, 2002.

Martha Minnow — *Breaking the Cycles of Hatred: Memory, Law, and Repair.* Princeton, NJ: Princeton University Press, 2002.

Barbara Perry — *In the Name of Hate: Understanding Hate Crimes.* New York: Routledge, 2000.

Barbara Perry, ed.

Hate and Bias Crimes: A Reader. New York: Routledge, 2003.

John W. Phillips

Sign of the Cross: The Prosecutor's True Story of a Landmark Trial Against the Klan. Louisville, KY: Westminster John Knox Press, 2000.

Chester L. Quarles

The Ku Klux Klan and Related American Racialist and Antisemitic Groups: A History and Analysis. Jefferson, NC: McFarland, 1999.

James Ridgeway

Blood in the Face: The Ku Klux Klan, Aryan Nations, Nazi Skinheads, and the Rise of a New White Culture. New York: Thunder's Mouth Press, 1995.

Ben Sonder

Militia Movement: Fighters of the Far Right. Danbury, CT: Franklin Watts, 2000.

Phillippa Strum

When the Nazis Came to Skokie. Lawrence: University Press of Kansas, 1999.

Dina Temple-Raston

A Death in Texas: A Story of Race, Murder, and a Small Town's Struggle for Redemption. New York: Henry Holt, 2003.

Jerome Walters

One Aryan Nation Under God: Exposing the New Racial Extremists. Cleveland: Pilgrim Press, 2000.

Index